★ ★ ★ ★ ★ ★ ★

Subs on the Hunt

40 of the Greatest WWII Submarine War Patrols

by
Richard G. Sheffield

CLUEfox Publishing – Atlanta, GA - 2009
© Copyright 2009 Richard Sheffield. All rights reserved.
First paperback edition 2009

© Copyright 2009 Richard Sheffield. Printed and bound in the United States of America. All rights reserved. No part of this publication may be reproduced, stored or transmitted in any form, for any reason or by any means, whether re-drawn, enlarged or otherwise altered including mechanical, photocopy, digital storage & retrieval or otherwise, without the prior permission in writing from both the copyright owner and the publisher (with the exception of a reviewer who may quote brief passages in a review to be printed in a newspaper or magazine).

The text, layout and designs presented in this book, as well as the book in its entirety, are protected by the copyright laws of the United States (17 U.S.C. 101 et seq.) and similar laws in other countries.

All photographs used with permission.

Courtesy of the National Archives.

Table of Contents

Foreword		**7**
1	The Submarine War	9
2	USS Triton: 3rd Patrol	29
3	S-44: 3rd Patrol	37
4	USS Guardfish: 1st Patrol	43
5	USS Guardfish 8th Patrol	51
6	USS Silversides: 4th Patrol	59
7	USS Silversides: 4th Patrol	67
8	USS Pogy: 5th Patrol	75
9	USS Wahoo: 3rd Patrol	81
10	USS Wahoo: 4th Patrol	91
11	USS Wahoo: 7th Patrol	103
12	USS Trigger: 6th Patrol	111
13	USS Seahorse 2nd Patrol	117
14	USS Seahorse 3rd Patrol	123
15	USS Seashorse 4th Patrol	129
16	USS Bowfin 2nd Patrol	137

17	USS Seawolf 12th Patrol	147
18	USS Snook 5th Patrol	153
19	USS Gunard 5th Patrol	159
20	USS Sandlance 2nd Patrol	165
21	USS Barb 8th Patrol	173
22	USS Barb 9th Patrol	181
23	USS Barb 11th Patrol	191
24	USS Harder 5th Patrol	199
25	USS Spadefish 1st Patrol	207
26	USS Spadefish 2nd Patrol	217
27	USS Spadefish 5th Patrol	223
28	USS Parche 2nd Patrol	233
29	USS Ray 5th Patrol	239
30	USS Ray 6th Patrol	247
31	USS Rasher 5th Patrol	257
32	USS Cabrilla 6th Patrol	263
33	USS Hammerhead 2nd Patrol	269
34	USS Atule 1st Patrol	275
35	USS Flasher 5th Patrol	281

36	USS Tirante 1st Patrol	287
37	USS Sea Dog 4th Patrol	295
38	USS Tang 1st Patrol	301
39	USS Tang 3rd Patrol	313
40	USS Tang 4th Patrol	333
41	USS Tang: 5th Patrol - Loss of the Tang	347

Glossary of Terms — *363*

Foreword

Read the remarkable tales of the brave captains' adventures as they slip in and out of the Emperor's dominion, claiming the high seas for their own. Follow the exploits of submarines like *S-44, Pogy, Wahoo, Snook, Gunard, Sandlance, Parche, Cabrilla, Atule, Flasher, Sea Dog, and Tang*. Learn about the strategies of the submarine war: attack basics and terminology, navigation, and common routes taken into and out of battle.

These are 40 of the best and most exciting adventures, following the day-to-day actions of the most successful combat submarine skippers. Watch with them as the big freighters go down, listen to the sound of shearing metal, and wait out the depth charge attacks in close, airless quarters, hundreds of feet underwater.

Share the thoughts and perceptions of legendary commanders like "Mush" Morton, Charles Kirkpatrick, J.R. "Dinty" Moore, Thomas Klakring, N.G. Ward, C.R. Burlingame, John S. Coye, and Dick O'Kane as they stalk their prey, wait in ambush, and face the rigors of failing equipment, unpredictable torpedoes, and ramming attempts by freighters and escorts.

This book is full of the stuff that makes heroes of ordinary men. See what it takes to match these adventures, attack for attack, using a simulator, the powers of the imagination, and these sterling examples of valor.

1 The Submarine War

The Japanese attack on Pearl Harbor launched the greatest naval war of all time. The attack was brilliantly timed and executed, but fatally flawed. Many say that failing to catch the U.S. carriers in port was the biggest error. Possibly so. In any case, the carriers weren't there to be attacked.

The U.S. Pacific submarine force was there however, and it was totally ignored. Hundreds of Japanese torpedo-plane pilots flew right over—and sometimes next to—the submarine base and it's munitions dump on neighboring Kuaha. In doing so, they missed a golden opportunity to destroy the one arm of the U.S. Navy capable of attacking the weakest link in the Empire's chain: shipping. Missing the subs may have been the fatal flaw.

Another Japanese Freighter Goes Down

Japan was an overpopulated island nation totally dependent on imports for everything from rice to oil. The large surface ships either damaged or destroyed at Pearl Harbor were impressive and powerful, but it would have been many months, or even years, before the ships could operate deep into Japanese controlled areas of the Pacific. However on the afternoon of the attack on Pearl Harbor, December 7, 1941, the order was given: *Execute unrestricted air and submarine warfare against Japan.* The subs, with their supplies and harbor facilities spared in the attack, were the only forces capable of responding immediately, and respond they did—slowly at first, but with gathering speed.

The year 1942 was a tentative one for the submarine forces. Outdated tactics had to be discarded, unaggressive skippers replaced, exploratory reconnaissance conducted, and new tactics developed. Only 139 ships were sunk by submarines in 1942, but the foundation was laid. With many of the tactical problems behind them, the U.S. submarine forces moved into 1943 with but one major problem: faulty torpedoes.

The year 1943 saw increasing numbers of successful patrols, most notably those of Commander Dudley "Mush" Morton and the USS *Wahoo*, whose outstanding patrols are described in detail in this book. His aggressive attacks gave the entire corps a lift just when they needed it.

Torpedo problems remained, highlighted by the experience of the USS *Tinosa*. On one occasion, the *Tinosa* intercepted and attacked a large tanker. Four torpedoes were fired, and although several appeared to hit the ship, only minor damage resulted. The tanker was stopped but not ready to sink. The submarine's captain, Commander Daspit, had a sitting duck and so moved in for the kill, conning the boat to a perfect firing position 875 yards away.

He fired nine torpedoes, one after another. All hit. All were duds. In all 15 shots were fired at the tanker; 13 hit their target, but after the attack, the ship was in no danger of sinking. The captain held onto his last torpedo and headed for home. A similar incident happened to the *Wahoo*.

Testing showed that the better the setup, the more likely it was that the torpedo would be a dud! The problem was the firing pin: If the torpedo struck the target at a perfect 90-degree angle, the firing pin would almost always shear off and the torpedo would fail to explode. Even with this serious torpedo problem, the 1943 total went up to 307 ships sunk.

The year 1944 would see the virtual destruction of the Japanese merchant fleet. By the end of the first half of 1944, the war in the Pacific was no longer in doubt. Three of the five Japanese aircraft carriers remaining at the beginning of the year were lying on the bottom—two of them downed by submarines. The "back" of the fleet was finally broken.

With the Japanese fleet severely depleted, the submarines turned their attention to the tankers carrying fuel oil for the fleet and aircraft. One tanker after another went to the bottom. Fuel became so critical that training missions for new pilots were severely cut, and as a result, the "green" Japanese pilots were easy pickings for the now-veteran U.S. naval aviators.

The USS *Tang*, under the command of Dick O'Kane, had her legendary run in 1944 (her entire career is set down in Chapters 38-41, so you can trace her path). With properly running torpedoes and many new boats in service, submarines sank 548 ships in 1944, effectively isolating Japan from the resources they needed to continue the war.

The year 1945 was a year of mopping up; still, one more major submarine offensive was needed to convince the Japanese leaders to give up the fight. Ships were being sunk faster than they could be replaced, and the pickings were getting slim. United States submarines hadn't ventured back in to the Sea of Japan since the *Wahoo* was lost there in 1943, but with new mine-detecting devices it was now time to reenter "Hirohito's Lake" and avenge the loss of the *Wahoo*.

Admiral Lockwood, COMSUBPAC, put together and ordered "Operation Barney." Nine fleet subs—the *Sea Dog, Crevalle, Spadefish, Tunny, Skate, Bonefish, Flyingfish, Bowfin*, and *Tinosa*—ventured into the Sea of Japan to show the Emperor that the U.S. had the capability of cutting him off from the mainland completely. The operation was a resounding success with 28 merchant ships and assorted others sunk, but unfortunately, the *Bonefish* didn't return. Going down with all hands, she was the last Pacific sub lost in the war.

Japanese Destroyer Torpedoed by the *Seawolf*

With the Empire on the verge of starvation, atomic bomb attacks on Japan several weeks later pushed the tiny empire off the edge. The result was surrender. While the crews of the "flat tops" and pilots stole most of the headlines, the submariners of the Silent Service carried the ball for much of the war. Although they numbered fewer than two percent of U.S. Navy personnel, these men accounted for well over half the ships sunk.

Attack Basics and Terminology

Submariners use terminology standards to all nautical activities. Some of the most common terms are:

Bow	The front or forward part of a ship.
Stern	The rear or *aft* part of a ship.
Starboard	The right side of a ship when facing forward.
Port	The left side of a ship when facing forward.
Quarter	An area off to one side of a ship; for example, the right rear area would be the *aft starboard quarter*.

Many of these terms will be used in the patrol section of this book while others, not listed here, will also be used from time to time. Those will be explained either at the time of mention or in the glossary at the end of the book.

A submarine attack is normally divided into three parts:

⇨ The *classification* phase
⇨ The *approach* phase
⇨ The *attack* phase

The classification phase consists of sighting a possible target and tracking it long enough to determine the target's direction of travel. Most games sight the targets for you, so all you have to do is determine the direction of travel. If the target is too far away for the game to make a determination for you, you can do it yourself by heading directly toward the contact.

Note the relative motion of the target to your heading. Its movement to your right or left will give you an idea of its direction. If it doesn't move in either direction, it's either moving directly toward or away from you.

The approach phase consists of moving to a firing position undetected by the enemy. After determining the target's course, you should determine if the target is ahead of or behind you. If he's ahead of you, most likely you'll need to perform an *end-around* maneuver to get ahead of him. This is normally executed on the surface to avoid running down your batteries; as such, you may need to pull away from the target to avoid being spotted when you surface.

If the target is behind you, you should use a *standard approach* course. This can be accomplished while you're submerged during the day or on the surface at night. The rule of thumb for a standard approach is to take an intercept course to the target track that is 90 degrees off the line of sight to the target. You should try to reach a firing position ahead of the enemy, off his track by 1000-2000 yards. It's best to get here ahead of him and wait in silent ambush, but you can attack on the move if it looks like the target may get by you.

The attack phase involves remaining undetected until time to fire, firing the torpedoes, and then withdrawing if necessary. If you're waiting in an ambush position, it's best to *point the target*—keep turning slightly so that as the target approaches, your bow is always pointing directly at him. That way, you always present a minimum angle to lookouts and sonar operators. Your best firing position is one in which the target will be at a perfect right angle to you when the torpedo hits. This will give you a wide broadside target.

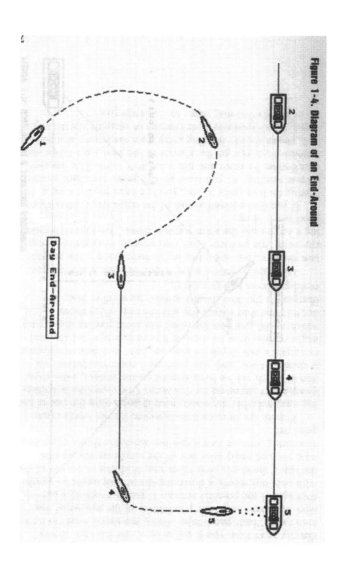

Diagram of an End-Around

Shooting at a target headed straight for you is called a *down-the-throat* shot. Conversely, shooting at a target headed directly away from you is called an *up-the-kilt* shot. These aren't very "high percentage" shots, but they'll work on occasion. You must weight the possibilities of the success of this shot against the possible returns. If you're attacking a convoy with only one escort, a down-the-throat shot might be worth the risk if the escort crew spots you. With the escort out of the way, you can easily take care of the whole convoy. In this case, firing three or four torpedoes down-the-throat might be a good risk.

If there are more escorts, however, it's not worth throwing away valuable torpedoes; your chances with the rest of the group aren't improved by this tactic. One exception is a situation in which you've been spotted on the surface, a destroyer is coming at you, and you know he'll reach you before you can attain a safe depth. In this case, one shot down-the-throat might hit him or at least cause him to turn to avoid the shot, which would give you the chance to avoid passing directly under him and thus reduce the effectiveness of his depth charges. By the time he gets around for another pass, you could get down to a safe depth.

There are countless other tactics, each designed for a certain situation, but one other worth mentioning is the *parallel approach*. One problem often encountered by captains is finding a way to use the stern torpedo tubes. This approach makes good use of them.

If you find yourself ahead of the target ship, rather than waiting for it to come to you, you can head toward it on a reverse heading. As you close on the target, turn hard in one direction or the other and fire your stern tubes; second, you're already heading away from the enemy at a good speed, which increases your chances of escaping the destroyers or escorts that may come to challenge you.

Diagram of a Down-the-Throat Shot

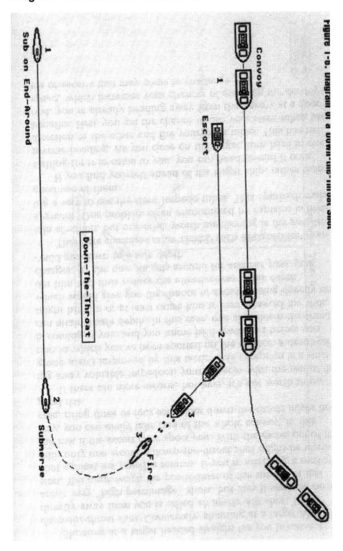

Diagram of a Parallel Approach

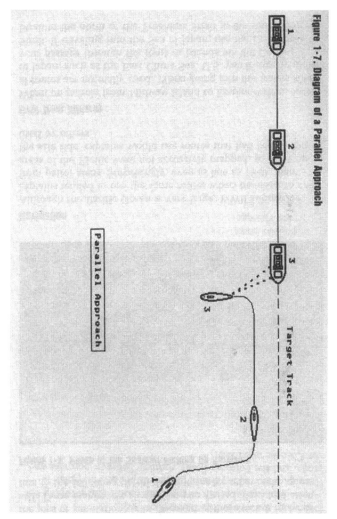

Figure 1-7. Diagram of a Parallel Approach

As mentioned, there are many other tactics, and one of the joys of simulations is in discovering those tactics for yourself. These maneuvers should get you started. Pay close attention to the following patrol descriptions for other techniques.

Navigation

Although the Pacific Ocean is very large, WWII submarine captains tended to use the same routes when traveling to and from patrol areas. Surprisingly, even as late as 1940 many areas of the Pacific were not accurately mapped, so to be on the safe side, captains would use routes that had been safely used by others.

Over from Midway

When on patrols from Midway Island to Empire waters, several routes are normally used. When going into the waters south of Japan, such as the East China Sea, you'll usually make your passage through the Ryukyu Islands via the Colnett Strait. If traveling into the Sea of Japan, use the La Pcʒrouse Strait to the north or the Tsushima Strait to the south. Entry into the Inland Sea is made through the Bungo Strait (made famous in the movie *Run Silent, Run Deep*).

A little farther south of the main routes and shipping bottlenecks is the Luzon Strait, just north of the Philippine Islands, and the Formosa Strait, running between Formosa and the Chinese mainland.

Up from Australia

When traveling north from Australia, the main route used is through the Lombok Strait or occasionally through the Sunda Strait. Once into the Java Sea, you would continue north through the Makassar Strait. In the Philippines area, you would use the Sibutu Passage or the Balabac Strait.

Figure 1-9. Travel Routes Map

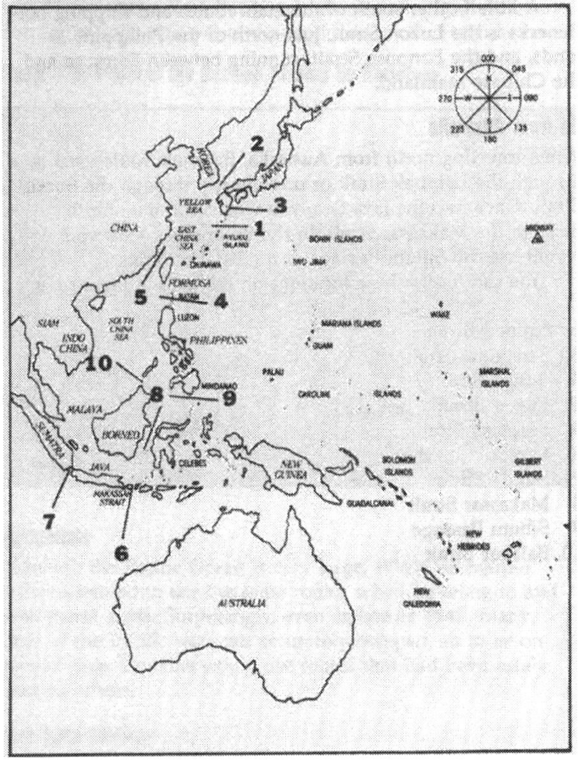

You can locate these locations on the map in the map above.

1. Colnett Strait
2. Tsushima Strait
3. Bungo Strait
4. Luzon Strait
5. Formose Strait

6. Lombok Strait
7. Sunda Strait
8. Makassar Strait
9. Sibutu Passage
10. Balabac Strait

2 USS Triton: 3rd Patrol

The first of the Pacific Fleet's submarines to cruise against the Japanese was the USS *Triton*; Her keel was laid at the U.S. Shipyard in Portsmouth, New Hampshire on 5 July 1939. On 15 August 1940, she was commissioned and quickly became a member of the pacific fleet. On 18 April 1942, Commander Charles Kirkpatrick took the boat out of Midway on her third combat patrol. It was his first patrol in command of the *Triton*.

Torpedo Attack #1

While the *Triton* was still a long way from the Japanese mainland, the watch sighted a large trawler near Marcus

Island, a Japanese stronghold. Captain Kirkpatrick fired two forward torpedoes from the surface and both missed. Not wishing to waste more torpedoes, the captain ordered the gun crew to the deck. They opened fire with both the deck gun and the 50-caliber machine gun. The trawler was quickly in flames and going down.

On 27 April, the *Triton* entered its patrol area near the Bonin Islands south of Japan. On 1 may, it moved into the East China Sea.

Torpedo Attack #2

That morning, smoke was sighted and a loosely formed convoy came into sight. The *Triton* had no trouble closing on the enemy track, and she approached submerged to a firing position. Captain Kirkpatrick fired two torpedoes at the leading freighter. They hit. Two more were fired at the second ship—both missed.

An escort turned and followed the wake of the first torpedo back to be starting point and dropped several depth charges, but none came close. By this time, the captain had taken the boat deep and moved around to the other side of the convoy. When it became obvious that he had evaded the escorts, Captain Kirkpatrick ordered the tubes reloaded as quietly as possible as he moved in from the other flank. The target of the first attack was still afloat but damaged. It seemed to be adrift and was being left behind. Kirkpatrick pulled to within 800 yards and put a torpedo from the stern tubes into the damaged ship. The explosion broke the ship's back and it sank in pieces.

Torpedo Attack #3

Early in the morning on 6 May, the *Triton* was making a surface patrol when a large dark shape appeared off the starboard bow. Soon, other vessels came into view and Captain Kirkpatrick began his approach. The escort ships couldn't be located so the commander assumed they were ahead and on the sides of the convoy. With this in mind, he decided to let the group pass and attack the tail end as it went by. The largest targets seemed to be to the rear of the group.

At 0245, the *Triton* fired two torpedoes at a large freighter in the rear of the convoy. The first shot failed to run—once free of the tube, it simply sank. The second shot missed ahead of the target. Since neither torpedo exploded and there was still no sign of the escorts, the submarine moved in again to attack.

Everything came together at once. An escort was seen bearing down, the escort crew saw the sub, and the freighter was in target position. The *Triton* fired two torpedoes and put on all four engines and pulled away from the escort. At least one torpedo hit with a resounding explosion that shook the boat several thousand yards away. The sub continued on the surface to regain a position ahead of the convoy.

Torpedo Attack #4

As dawn was approaching, Captain Kirkpatrick maneuvered his sub into a satisfactory position and waited for the ships to come to him. When the convoy passed, he fired two torpedoes each at the third and fourth ships. The third ship took a hit and started to list, but the fourth ship was able to turn and avoid the torpedoes.

Now that the sub had been sighted, the captain took the boat down to 90 feet and crossed under the middle of the convoy in an attempt to lose the escorts. The destroyers closed and dropped a number of depth charges, but they caused no damage. When the Triton was able to return to periscope depth, the convoy had moved on, and the sub couldn't catch it.

The next several days were spent crossing the China Sea and looking for traffic in the shipping lanes, but none was sighted. On 14 May, the sub intercepted a message from Task Force Seven relaying information about a possible carrier in the area toward which they were headed. Although he wasn't directly ordered to intercept, Captain Kirkpatrick decided to look for the carrier group during the search, he came upon two large fishing boats and sank them with the deck gun. He only had one torpedo forward and four aft.

While the sub was patrolling submerged on 16 May, the Enemy carrier group seemed to "pop out of the haze." The *Triton* tried to approach, but it was difficult to do so submerged. Once, Kirkpatrick closed the gap, but by the time he could turn to bring the stern tubes to bear, the carrier had moved out to 9000 yards.

The *Triton* tried to follow as best she could but finally lost contact. When Commander Kirkpatrick saw the quarry was lost, he ordered the boat to surface and broadcast the contact report, hoping someone else could catch the carrier group.

Torpedo Attack #5

While the *Triton* was working her way back toward the Bonin Islands, a Japanese sub suddenly appeared at 6200 yards. This would be a real trophy to bag, so Kirkpatrick approached cautiously.

He ordered two torpedoes fired, resulting in one hit at the rear of the enemy boat. The explosion blew the stern section 100 feet into the air and the sub sank by the stern as the crew scrambled out. Another attack was made using the stern tubes on the way back to Midway, but no hits were scored.

The USS *Triton's* career was cut short when she failed to report in during her 6th war patrol: When she failed to return to Australia on time, she was presumed lost. It was not until after the war that the results of their 6th patrol and her fate were learned. She had been tracking a convoy on 6 March 1943 and had made a successful attack, sinking a 3000-ton freighter. She continued to track this group for several days and was probably making another attack when after a severe depth charge attack, pieces of wood, cork, and a great quantity of oil surfaced. It appears that the Triton was lost in battle off the Japanese coast on 15 March 1943.

3 S-44: 3ʳᵈ Patrol

The activities of the S-Boats, or sugar-boats as they were called, will long live in submarine history. Comparatively tiny World War I-era boats like the S-Boats were outdated by the time the U.S Navy went to war. However, the S-Boats' efforts undeniably influenced the war in the Pacific. That they could participate at all was nothing short of miraculous. They were designed to operate close to shore and in shallow water, and yet were asked to cross the vast Pacific Ocean—no one knew if S-Boats would survive the 12,000-mile run. Operated out of Brisbane, Australia, they made up Task Force 42. The most famous member of the group was *S-44*.

Although her war career was brief, few subs could match the courage and aggressive attacks of *S-44*. She was authorized in 1916 and finally commissioned in 1925. The S-Boats were very small—only 850 tons—had only four forward tubes and no rear torpedo tubes, could dive only to shallow depths, had only two engines, was slow on the surface, had no air conditioning, and seemed to leave an oil slick wherever she went. In addition to those basic design problems, most of the S-Boats were old and just about worn out.

The *S-44's* best trip out was her third war patrol, which started on 24 July 1942 at Brisbane, where she battled bad weather on the trip to the patrol area, the Solomon Sea. The captain was Lt. Commander J.R. "Dinty" Moore.

The watch sighted several ships in the patrol area, but Captain Moore was unable to close in to attack because of the boat's slow speed. Fate, however, placed *S-44* in the proper position on 10 August.

It so happened that on the previous day the Japanese had attacked the U.S. Navy forces around Sao with four heavy cruisers. Circling around the island, they made a surprise attack and dealt the Allied forces a severe set back: Four U.S. cruisers and one Australian cruiser sank with only minor damage to the Japanese ships. But on this day, the *S-44* would dampen the victory party aboard the withdrawing Japanese ships.

At 0750 on 10 August, four heavy cruisers were sighted heading toward the sub. The *S-44* was submerged. She quickly turned to open the distance to the target track. The captain stopped and set up for the attack from a scant 700 yards. He let most of the group pass as he waited to attack the last ship. When the last cruiser arrived, he fired four torpedoes and headed for 130 feet.

After a short run of only 35 seconds, four hard torpedo hits were heard, followed by a boiler explosion, and the sounds of a ship breaking up and heading for the bottom. And so ended the story of the first major Japanese warship, the 8800-ton *Kako*, sunk by a lone submarine attack.

A surprisingly short depth charge attack followed, but none were close. Apparently, the cruisers were more concerned with getting away from the sub than attacking her. The significance of the *Kako's* sinking is much larger than is apparent at first: During that time, the fate of the Marines on Guadalcanal hung in the balance. The second Japanese attack was certainly delayed by the threat of a large U.S. submarine force in the area, which was, in fact, only one lonely but brave sugar boat.

Aggressive attacks would be both the hallmark and the end of *S-44*: She was the only S-Boat in the Pacific to be lost due to enemy action. On 26 September 1943, she left on her fifth war patrol, under the command of Lt. Commander F.E. Brown, and she was never heard from again.

The story of her fate was finally learned upon the release of two surviving crewmen from the Japanese prison camps, where they spent the remainder of the war. She was patrolling on the surface when a plane forced her down by dropping several depth charges. When she surfaced, she made radar contact with what seemed to be a small merchant ship. Captain Brown approached on the surface and called for the gun crew. At close range, the gun crew opened fire.

The fire was immediately returned. The target turned out to be a destroyer. Totally outgunned, *S-44* took hits right away. The captain ordered her down, but then a shell hit the control room and the order couldn't be carried out. With the situation lost, the captain ordered the executive officer to wave a pillow case to signal surrender.

Although the flag of surrender could be seen plainly in the beam of his powerful searchlight, the captain of the destroyer continued to fire. As the boat began to sink, the crew tried to abandon ship, but only eight crew members made it into the water before the ship went down. Two of them survived in the 47-degree water long enough to be picked up by the destroyer.

4 USS Guardfish: 1ˢᵗ Patrol

After the war began, the USS *Guardfish* was one of the first new boats to enter the fleet. Built by the Electric Boat Company in Groton, Connecticut, she was launched on 20 January 1942.

Training was the first order of business for the new crew was they headed out of Pearl Harbor en route to the U.S. base on Midway. The drilling was continuous as Commander Thomas Klakring molded the group of young men into a fighting unit. The results of this training became evident soon after the *Guardfish* sailed from Midway on 7 August 1942.

Torpedo Attack #1

Her first encounter with the enemy came on 19 August off the coast of Japan near Tokyo. A freighter came into view with one escort. Just before dawn the *Guardfish* made her attack submerged. Captain Klakring fired three torpedoes at the target and headed down. Two good hits were heard, but a periscope check showed the ship undamaged and increasing speed. A closing destroyer and the coming dawn made further attacks impossible.

Over the next several days, the *Guardfish* patrolled the northern coast of Honshu. She made contact with, and then avoided, a number of patrol boats; several trawlers were located and sunk with the deck gun.

Torpedo Attack # 2

On 24 August, the *Guardfish* had better luck. A good-sized freighter was seen coming out of a harbor. At 1657, three torpedoes were fired at the ship from 1200 yards, resulting in two hits. This time, there was no doubt that the ship was damaged. The bow was blown off completely. The target sank vertically, bow-first, with the screws still turning as she went under.

Captain Klakring cleared the area to head up the coast to try to catch a group of ships seen heading that way. A near collision with a sampan foiled his plan. The sampan must have radioed the Guardfish's position because when the *Guardfish* arrived, the ships were nowhere to be found.

Torpedo Attack # 3

On the following morning, around dawn, the Guardfish contacted another lone freighter, and Captain Klakring fired two torpedoes from 1400 yards. The first hit right under the stack, but the second was erratic. The captain watched through the periscope as this torpedo made a series of 12-foot leaps into the air and then passed behind the target. The target was settling somewhat but not sinking. It was slowly making its way close to shore. As the Guardfish surfaced to give chase, radar picked up four planes and Captain Klakring ordered the boat to submerge again. The target successfully escaped to the shore.

The day and night of 26 August was spent playing tag with a tenacious patrol boat that followed, possibly with the aid of radar.

Torpedo Attack # 4

Early September was a bad time to be at sea northwest of Japan. The weather turned foul and Captain Klakring spent several days preoccupied with just keeping his boat afloat. Even at 150 feet the sea still moved the boat several degrees.

When the Guardfish was again patrolling the surface in very heavy seas on 2 September, the watch sighted a freighter at a range of eight miles. The sub put on speed to get ahead of her and at 0727 she submerged and moved in for the attack. Three torpedoes were fired for two hits; after the third torpedo it appeared to take on a list, but wasn't sinking, so the captain fired another torpedo. It's track couldn't be seen through the periscope and it wasn't heard from again.

At 0850, the crew of the freighter began to abandon ship. Suddenly, the target broke cleanly in half and sank in pieces. Several patrol vessels were heard approaching, so Klakring cleared the area, submerged and then surfaced to put some miles behind him.

Torpedo Attack # 5

The Guardfish's attacks continued along the northern coast of Honshu on 4 September as she tracked two freighters about half a mile offshore. Due to a strong current the sub wasn't able to close and, finally, the captain ordered a long-range shot from 5000 yards. Only one torpedo was fired, but it missed as the ship headed away to safety.

Torpedo Attack # 6

Later that afternoon the Guardfish wandered into the path of two large ore carriers. Captain Klakring ordered a quick setup with the stern tubes. At 1744, the captain fired one torpedo at the first ship and two at the second, resulting in a hit on each ship. The targets were heavily laden and each sank in less than ten minutes. As they went down, several other freighters came over the horizon then turned and headed away. The Guardfish was clearly having an effect on shipping in the area.

Torpedo Attack # 7

One of the escaping freighters moved into a harbor and dropped anchor, probably to wait for the cover of darkness. But Captain Klakring and his crew were feeling confident. They decided to try a long-range shot. The Guardfish moved quietly to within 6500 yards of the sitting ship and fired one torpedo. After a seven-minute and 20-second wait, the ship was struck amidships with a terrific explosion. The officers and crew were permitted to watch the ship sink through the periscope. This was one of the longest successful torpedo shots of the war.

Torpedo Attack # 8

During the attack on the anchored ship, another freighter appeared. With the ship in the harbor sinking nicely and escorts heading to greet it, the Guardfish moved at high speed to take the new target.

It turned out to be another ore ship. Captain Klakring moved in close on the surface and fired two torpedoes from 1000 yards. One hit just under the bridge and the freighter started to settle. Another shot was fired on a quick setup. It missed. The ore carrier's crew was already jumping from the ship, and it sank with the stern pointing straight up toward the sky. The fourth sinking of the day occurred a mile off shore.

There was a light depth charge attack, but as soon as all was quiet, the Guardfish surfaced and slid out of the area and eventually returned to Midway.

5 USS Guardfish 8th Patrol

The Guardfish left Midway on 18 June 1944 under the command of Lt. Commander N.G. Ward to patrol in the South China Sea, Luzon Straits area. The first few days on patrol were spent on rescue duty or repairing small problems that had developed. Aircraft contacts kept them on their toes, but no shipping was spotted until 5 July. Distant explosions were heard, but the Guardfish couldn't get in on the action due to constant air leaks, which continued to attract aircraft.

On 11 July, Lt. Commander Ward received a contact report form the USS Thrasher and opened up the engines to try to intercept. They made radar contact with the convoy at 20,000 yards and commenced a wide end-around to gain a firing position ahead of the group.

The convoy consisted of nine ships and at least five escorts. The watch made visual contact shortly after midnight, and by 0300, the Guardfish was in good attack position.

The half moon was right, preventing a surface attack, so Captain Ward dove at 0331 when the convoy was 17,000 yards way. At 9000 yards, the group made a wide zig that went undetected by the tracking party. When they looked up again, the firing range was a long 3800 yards. They made a quick adjustment to close the gap but were unsuccessful.

At 0512, the Guardfish surfaced to try another end-around. Distant explosions were again heard and planes drove them down, and when they came back up, the convoy was nowhere to be found. Once again, they were beaten to the punch.

Torpedo Attack # 1

At 0335, on 16 July 1944, another contact report was received and again Captain Ward raced to intercept. By 0945, the crew had located the convoy and started an end-around. Throughout the afternoon, they dove to avoid planes, but the loud pinging of the escorts always allowed them to keep track of the convoy. At 2235, they were in position 11,000 yards from the convoy—ten ships with three escorts.

The Guardfish let the escort slip past, and then at 2342, the captain fired all six forward torpedoes at five overlapping ships from 3300 yards. Guardfish swung hard to the right to attempt a shot on the next group with the stern tubes. All six shots then hit among four ships. A large tanker blew sky-high on impact, throwing flames thousands of feet into the air. A large freighter, presumed to be loaded with combustibles, also blew up. The third ship in line, a medium freighter, broke in two at the middle and sank, and the fourth ship went down by the bow. Four ships down with one salvo!

The other ships then scattered, making a follow-up shot impossible. Captain Ward picked a large target on the radar and began to track. Eventually the sub caught up with the freighter and swung around to use the stern tubes. Three torpedoes were fired, resulting in two hits. An escort was seen coming on hard, and as the Guardfish withdrew from the scene to reload, the target rolled over on its side and disappeared.

Another target appeared, heading towards the Guardfish. Captain Ward again set up for a stern shot and fired two torpedoes—a little early—at 2500 yards. Right after firing, the target made another large zig and both torpedoes missed. Moving ahead at flank speed, the Guardfish turned hard while making two bow tubes ready. Tubes 3 and 4 were fired from 1250 yards, both resulting in hits. A close escort and arising moon forced the *Guardfish* to retreat once again. The target started to settle and disappeared from radar at 13,000 yards. It's believed to have sunk but Ward only claimed damage.

Torpedo Attack # 2

The next afternoon, 17 July, the tracking team was back in business as a ship came into view at 12,000 yards. It soon became clear that it was part of a large, fast-moving convoy. The captain had to act fast or miss the opportunity. At least two aircraft carriers were seen as well as two tankers, but a large freighter was the closest target, so he chose it. With sound conditions very bad and the seas high, he approached two-thirds speed, making frequent periscope observations. He fired three bow torpedoes at the closest target: range 1370 yards, 75 port track, gyros 0.

Ward was setting up on a tanker when the first hit was heard, followed by a second. He swung the periscope back to see the freighter hit amidships, sinking fast. When he swung back to the tanker, it had changed course. A shot would have been impossible so he went deep and waited out the short depth charge attack. Back at periscope depth, Ward saw that the convoy was gone and an escort was circling the area of the attack, presumably picking up survivors. No chase of the remainder of the convoy was possible due to the state of the seas and dwindling fuel supply.

Torpedo Attack # 3

Ship contact was made on the SJ radar at 22,000 yards on 19 July 1944. Captain Ward ordered his crew to battle stations. Rainsqualls made tracking difficult and forced the Guardfish to dive early to avoid detection. The sub made periscope contact again at 0639, and Ward was pleased to see that the convoy had made an obliging turn in his direction.

A large, modern freighter was selected as the target, but the submarine was forced to submerge to 120 feet to duck under an escort. By the time the sub returned to the surface, the target had moved past and was presenting an unfavorable angle on the bow of 130 degrees. The captain lined up the next target and once again discovered he was fortunate enough to have overlapping targets at 1000 and 1500 yards. He fired the last four forward fish.

The first ship took two hits, one amidships and one forward; she broke in half immediately. The second ship took one hit, but the last torpedo was heard to pass back over the Guardfish after a dangerous circular run. Since depth control was having a hard time, the captain ordered deep water.

The first two depth charges were very close and shook things quite a bit. Two escorts made a systematic search, but the Guardfish quietly slid away. Since his boat was low on fuel, had few remaining torpedoes, and was leaking water in several places, Ward decided to head for home. The submarine arrived back at Midway on 31 July 1944.

Commander Ward executed some fine shooting on this trip and was lucky to escape the circular run of that last torpedo—others would not be so fortunate. In his report to his superior, Ward claimed seven sinkings for 50,700 tons. Ward and the crew were awarded the Presidential Unit Citation for their efforts. After the war, investigation reduced the total, but left it at a respectable four ships for 20,400 tons sunk.

6 USS Silversides: 4th Patrol

The Silversides was one of a handful of valiant boats to see the entire war. She made her first patrol early in 1942 and her last in 1945, and she was quite active in between, tallying 13 patrols by the war's end.

Some of the patrols examined so far are examples of what can happen when things are going your way, but the fourth patrol of the Silversides is an example of just how much can be accomplished when everything seems to be going wrong. With outstanding courage and fortitude, the men of the Silversides beat the odds and turned in an outstanding patrol even though the trip had a very rocky start.

On 17 December 1943, the Silversides departed Brisbane, Australia under the command of Commander C.R. Burlingame. Her mission was to patrol in the area of Truk Island. Without the usual training period, the sub immediately headed for the assigned area.

Torpedo Attack # 1

While Silversides was still en route, on 23 December, the watch spotted what appeared to be a submarine. As the boat was close to the edge of her boundary, the captain assumed the sub was friendly and tried to work his way around it, but as the Silversides passed between the sub and the low moon the dim shape suddenly turned towards them. Flank speed was ordered, but even at 20 knots, the Silversides was going to be overtaken.

In desperation, the captain tried to signal the boat to determine if it was indeed friendly or not. The answer to their signal was not Morse code, so two stern torpedoes were sent down the throat of what turned out to be a small destroyer. The first exploded prematurely and the second was never heard from, so Commander

Burlingame took the boat deep and rigged for depth charges. After the destroyer made a couple of runs over the sub with no damage, the captain ordered the boat back to periscope depth. The target was sighted but approach was impossible.

Later, at about 0900, just after a periscope sweep, a Japanese bomber dropped three large bombs directly on top of them in rapid succession. Every light in the forward torpedo room and the conning tower was knocked out, and men were thrown off their feet and out of their bunks. Many were cut by broken glass. Burlingame ordered the sub down and quickly found the bow planes to be jammed on hard dive. After 15 difficult minutes, the depth was stabilized and the boat brought under control. They had taken quite a beating and had yet to make an approach.

Torpedo Attack # 2

Life was slow and easy for several days as the Silversides made her way to Truk. All possible repairs were made; then, suddenly, late in the afternoon on 6 January, a large enemy sub appeared 5000 yards off the starboard quarter. The Silversides turned quickly and fired three torpedoes. Again, the first went off too soon but the second struck the target and stopped her dead in the water.

The captain ordered a dive after firing to avoid the almost inevitable air search that would follow. The Silversides only received credit for damaging the enemy sub, but it's quite likely that she either sank or was put totally out of commission.

Torpedo Attack # 3

A tanker was spotted on 7 January, the following day, but it zigged away and couldn't be tracked. The crew of the Silversides agonized over missing the opportunity, but a second chance came on 18 January, when another tanker was sighted at 0100.

This time the captain was able to gain a marvelous firing position ahead of the target. He slowed the sub and turned her to bring the stern tubes to bear. At 0255, four stern shots were fired with very satisfactory results. Burlingame described it as "A tremendous explosion and pillar of black smoke 200 feet high, flame and sparks at its base and out the stack."

Evasive action began: The sound man listened to the sounds of the tanker breaking up; escorts quickly arrived and dropped a series of charges—the first barrage blew the gasket off a safety vent. Air had to be added to one of the safety tanks, but the air went straight to the surface instead. The escort used this convenient marker to drop another series of "tooth shakers" on Silversides.

The escort finally left, but later, a plane located the sub and dropped a bomb. Fortunately, it missed astern. An oil leak explained how the plane found them. Fuel had to be transferred out of the leaking tank, and the list of damaged or unworkable equipment grew.

Torpedo Attack # 4

Undaunted, the captain pursued a group of three warships the following day but couldn't close for an attack. This chase led them outside the assigned area so they turned and headed back to Truk. While the sub was traveling on the surface on 20 January, a watch spotted smoke. The sub trailed four good-sized freighters with two escorts, one in front and one in the rear. After following them for about six hours, the captain knew the convoy's base course and zig pattern. With this information in hand, he pulled ahead of the group to attack at dusk.

The convoy was silhouetted against the setting sun. Silversides closed in for the kill as the ships took a zig in the opposite direction. The convoy presented itself at such an angle that three ships were lined up bow to stern, forming a huge target. Even tough the range was over 4000 yards, the chance for a hit was quite good and the captain ordered all six forward torpedoes fired.

The sub immediately went deep to avoid the escorts. Five good torpedo hits were heard and all three ships were hit. Explosions and the sound of ships breaking up were heard as the escorts closed in. The depth charges fell but none appeared to cause serious damage; however, one of the torpedo doors was jammed open and the sub developed an air leak.

The Silversides later surfaced and left the area at full speed. A man was put overboard to assess the damage to the jammed door only to find torpedo number 6 still stuck in the tube, half in and half out. Another fuel leak was discovered and the air leak was still unaccounted for. Shortly after starting ahead again, an explosion occurred in the main generator, breakdown of the induction operating gear revealed a box of breakfast food under the bell crank lever.

Thus, with a dangling torpedo with warhead attached, a fuel leak, an air leak, an explosion in the generator, and Cream of Wheat® in the main induction, the sub turned toward home a little early, headed for Pearl Harbor.

Upon its return, the Silversides was given credit only for damaging the target ships since they had not actually seen the ships sink. But shortly thereafter, intelligence reports confirmed the sinkings and Burlingame was credited with sinking four ships for a tonnage total of 27,798.

7 USS Silversides: 4*th* *Patrol*

By the time Silversides' 10th patrol rolled around, she was under the capable command of John S. Coye. With a couple of patrols already under his belt, Coye was about to reach his stride. On 26 April 1944, he set out from Brisbane, Australia to patrol the area round the Marianas Islands.

Torpedo Attack # 1

On 8 May, he made landfall on Guam and immediately noticed almost continuous air activity. Shortly after noon, a large group of ships was sighted heading in the direction of the sub. A short run put Silversides just off the target track and she moved in submerged.

The convoy consisted of six or seven ships in a rough formation of three columns. Five escorts were also sighted, three of which were the Chidori class. An unfavorable zig left Coye in a bad position for a bow shot, so he quickly turned the boat and fired all four stern tubes on a 5000-ton transport ship and took the sub down deep, anticipating a strong reaction by the escorts.

One hit was reported, but a sinking could not be confirmed. The escorts milled about for a while, dropping a few depth charges here and there, but they never had a good fix on the Silversides. The sub surfaced after dark and again noted air activity over Guam.

Torpedo Attack # 2

At 0821 the following morning, a seven-ship convoy was spotted heading out of the harbor toward Japan. The ships formed up into three columns and headed out to sea. Coye tried his best to close to a firing position, but being so close to the air base on Guam, he had to remain submerged. Late that afternoon, with the batteries well down, he surfaced and looked for the convoy's smoke. He regained contact with the ships and increased speed to overtake them. Tracking was difficult as the radar chose this moment to break down.

A wide end-around was executed to put Silversides in a good position ahead of the group. At twilight, she dove for the attack. The ships had just finished a zig, which put the sub in a good position for a shot on their flank; many ships were overlapping. John Coye ordered six torpedoes fired, resulting in five hits. He took the sub deep and rigged for depth charges.

The escorts dropped several charges, but not close enough to cause concern. The sub headed back up to periscope depth. One ship had already sunk and another was in flames. The captain let the entire crew have a look and take pictures.

They waited until the following morning for the other ship to sink. She kept hanging on despite the fact that she seemed on the verge of going down. That afternoon, as the captain ordered the crew to prepare a torpedo to finish her off, the smoldering ship silently slipped under the waves.

Coye chased the remainder of the convoy during the night, but just as he came in for the attack, the moon clouded over and the ships couldn't be seen. By the time light conditions improved, the convoy had slipped past. Dawn was approaching and Guam was still within sight, so he couldn't follow on the surface.

Torpedo Attack # 3

During a patrol off Saipan, the Silversides sighted smoke, and closed in for a look. What looked to be a large convoy turned out to be two sub-hunting ships, putting out a good bit of "come hither" smoke to attract unsuspecting subs. Coye cleared the area without detection. The next day he again had to avoid this pair as they wandered around the area.

The next several days were spent patrolling the Guam-to-Saipan route. Finally, on the afternoon of 20 May, smoke was sighted coming toward the sub. A cautious approach revealed a single transport with at least four escorts.

Undaunted by the odds, Coye closed in for the kill. At a range of 1600 yards—close for a daylight attack—Coye fired four torpedoes at the transport. Two good hits were heard as he ordered a dive. He left the surface none too soon: The escorts and air support let them have it. Due to the shallow water the sub could find nowhere to hide. Coye kept his speed up and tried to avoid the attack. In all, 61 depth charges were dropped, including one salvo of 24 dropped in rapid succession. The soundman thought he could hear the sound of the target breaking up, but he couldn't be sure because the depth charges drowned out everything.

Silversides surface later for a quick look and came face to face with another escort. The captain had to go deep for another hour. Finally, around 2:00 the sub surfaced and cleared the area. Again, several days passed with little action.

Torpedo Attack # 4

Early in the morning on 28 May 1944, a group of ships came over the horizon and headed straight for the sub.

Coye and crew tracked the convoy from ahead for a while and decided that due to the glassy calm surface of the water, they would wait until after dark to attack.

Later that afternoon, he let the group go by and gave it a good looking over. The group consisted of two freighters and four escorts. When night fell, the sub surfaced and pursued.

At midnight, the moon set and Coye moved in closer on the surface. As he was setting up the shot, an escort tuned in the direction of the sub. Feeling that long shot was better than no shot at all, he fired six torpedoes—three at each target from a range of 3400 yards. He watched as both ships took two hits each and exploded. The flames lit the whole area as bright as day. Still on the surface, the sub pulled away at emergency speed and watched the ships burn. Apparently the ships were loaded with gasoline and, "a million or so gallons burning is truly an awe-inspiring spectacle."

After this busy period, the boat headed north past Asuncion Island, and after one more unsuccessful attack, the captain ordered a course back to Pearl Harbor because he was out of torpedoes.

Silversides was initially given credit for sinking five ships for at total of 23,600 tons. These figures were eventually revised to show six ships sunk for a total of 14,141. The extra ship, however, should have pleased Coye as it moved him into a small group of only eight commanders who sank six or more ships in one patrol.

8 USS Pogy: 5th Patrol

The keel for the USS Pogy was laid at Manitowoc Shipyards in Wisconsin in September 1941. It was the start of a long and distinguished performance record. She left for her first war patrol in January 1943 and continued to patrol enemy waters until the end of the war. Her 10^{th,} and final, patrol in August 1945. Along the way, she sent over **60,000** tons of Japanese shipping to the bottom. Perhaps her finest hour came during her 5th patrol in February 1944.

Her 5th patrol sent her west from Midway to conduct an anti-shipping sweep of the coast of Formosa. Seas were rough during her trip to the area, but she sill arrived a little ahead of schedule.

Torpedo Attack # 1

Once the Pogy moved into her assigned area, the watch immediately contacted a six-ship convoy. A night surface approach seemed out of the question due to the excellent visibility and watchful eye of three well-placed escort vessels. The captain, Commander R. M. Metcalf, decided to track the group for a while. The group moved in close to shore; then one ship moved away from the group with no escort. The Pogy began to track this lone ship and moved in to attack.

The target was making 11 knots and the Pogy was heading in at a similar speed. At a range of 2500 yards, she fired three torpedoes, but the target saw the sub and made a quick course change. All the torpedoes missed. The captain decided that if he were to follow the lone ship for another attack, he wouldn't have time to catch and attack the other component of the convoy. So he broke off the attack and changed course.

Torpedo Attack # 2

By the time the submarine caught up with the other ships, a heavy mist had set in which reduced visibility to about 3500 yards. The captain maneuvered Pogy to a position about 10,000 yards ahead of the group and then turned to head directly toward them on an opposite heading.

As the first ship approached, he turned the boat to head in on its flank. When the target came into view, it was immediately apparent that it was not a freighter at all but a dangerous-looking destroyer. A quick order was given to change torpedo settings to run shallow and two fish were fired. A large freighter came into view and three shots were fired at it.

Then the situation became "rather confused," as the two torpedoes hit and the destroyer completely exploded. Two torpedoes hit the second ship as well, and it sank in about a minute. Then, a torpedo was heard running toward the sub!
The captain attempted to turn to use the stern tubes on another ship, but instead of running, this target turned with the clear intention of attempting to ram the Pogy.

She put on four engines and slowly pulled away while the crew of the freighter shot at the sub with everything from pistols to a four-inch gun. Metcalf was so engrossed in watching the display that he missed a golden opportunity for a down-the-throat shot, for at one point, the freighter was only 800 yards away.

Torpedo Attack # 3

On 13 February, a target was spotted on radar at 20,000 yards, and the sub moved in to check it out. At first, it appeared to be dead in the water; later, Commander Metcalf saw that it was a damaged freighter with two escorts, moving at two knots. Metcalf moved in for a shot, and just before dawn, he fired two torpedoes. Both ran erratically and neither hit the target. Heavy seas prevented a second attack so the Pogy moved out to open water to reload.

Torpedo Attack # 4

Fifteen minutes after midnight on 20 February, the sub contacted another convoy at 20000 yards. Pogy moved ahead of the group and waited for it to approach. As the convoy came closer, Metcalf headed slowly toward the two target ships. When the range was 3000 yards, the targets made a zig toward the Pogy and Metcalf stopped the boat and set up to shoot. At a range of 1300 yards, he fired two torpedoes. One hit. The freighter went to the bottom, still under power, in 52 seconds.

Several hours later, the Pogy caught up with the second target ship. The captain managed to put one torpedo into it, but it pulled away and wasn't seen to sink. Another attack several days later had similar results with only one ship damaged.

Torpedo Attack # 5

On 23 February, Metcalf caught up with a convoy he had tried to attack the night before with limited success. A first attack attempt netted them zero hits after six shots, but Metcalf wouldn't give up. He pulled ahead of the group and made a surface approach.

At about 3500 yards, the convoy made a convenient zig towards the Pogy so she just stopped and waited. At 2600 yards, she turned and fired all four stern tubes at a large freighter. Torpedoes number 8 and number 9 hit with normal explosions and Pogy pulled away from the area. As they were leaving the area at 0449, the bridge crew saw the freighter sink with its bow pointing straight up.

Now with only one torpedo left, the Pogy headed for home. She made a short stop at Rasa Island to use the deck gun to bombard a large phosphate plant there, but with limited success. That out of their system, the crew of the Pogy headed back to Midway.

9 USS Wahoo: 3rd Patrol

As the year 1942 came to a close, many of the older submarine commanders who started the war were being replaced by younger, more aggressive skippers. Such was the case with the Wahoo. Her first two patrols had been ineffective and frustrating for the crew and officers—the captain was of the old school and continued to follow the pre-war attack doctrine that was rapidly proving to be too cautious. So, after riding along as an observer and prospective commanding officer on the previous patrol, Captain Dudley W. (Mush) Morton took command on 31 December 1942.

Before even leaving the dock, Morton made his intentions clear with regard to the coming patrol: In each compartment, he placed placards that read in beg red letters, SHOOT THE SONS OF BITCHES. A brief meeting was held and Morton explained that they would carefully check each contact, and if it proved to be an enemy ship, they would attack until it was on the bottom. Period.

Now with a rejuvenated crew, the Wahoo headed out from Brisbane, Australia on 15 January 1943. Her orders were to conduct training exercises with the U.S. destroyer Patterson for several days, and then proceed on to the Palau Islands through the Vitiaz Strait, which runs between New Guinea and New Britain.

Torpedo Attack # 1

Training went well, and by the morning of 24 January, Wahoo was deep into the Solomon Sea, approaching the strait. While the captain was investigating an anchorage near Karsu Island, several ships were spotted in the harbor. As Morton conned the boat to a good attack position, a destroyer appeared. While he was certain the Wahoo hadn't been spotted, he couldn't ignore the approaching destroyer without endangering the boat.

Morton gave the order to switch targets and rapidly the officers began to plot the attack. With but a quick chance for a setup, Executive Officer O'Kane gave the order, and three torpedoes were fired. It was immediately obvious to O'Kane that they had misread the speed and that all three fish would shoot behind the target. He increased the speed estimate and fired one more shot, but the lookouts on the destroyer were now alert and the ship turned in time to avoid the torpedo, the destroyer continued its turn and was then headed directly toward the Wahoo. The crew was only slightly surprised when Morton said they would ignore the standing doctrine, which called for the Wahoo to dive in such a situation, and attempt a down-the-throat shot.

O'Kane fed readings to the captain and conned the destroyer so that it was dead ahead. As the range narrowed past 1200 yards, the first torpedo was fired. Another set of readings and the second was away—with the range only 750 yards! The Wahoo headed for the bottom and rigged for depth charges.

The sound of exploding depth charges was followed by a much louder explosion and the sound of cracking as hot boilers came into contact with seawater. They had scored a hit! A quick pop-up to periscope depth revealed a sinking destroyer with the crew abandoning ship. Not bad for a first engagement. They slowly made their way out of the area.

Torpedo Attack # 2

Now clear of the straits and headed northwest, the Wahoo settled into a normal patrol routine. Just before breakfast on 26 January, the routine was interrupted by the call of "smoke on the horizon." Morton kept her on the surface and determined the makeup of the convoy. He was in luck: It was a large convoy with no apparent escort ship. Morton concluded that the destroyer they sank two days earlier must have been headed out to meet this group. Still on the surface, the captain took the boat to a position well ahead of the convoy and waited. At last, the tops of the masts appeared over the horizon and Morton ordered the Wahoo down.

The Wahoo Sinks the Dakar Maru

O'Kane, at the periscope, called out the range and described each ship. Then as they prepared to open fire, the convoy took a sudden zig toward them. The target track was now too close for the torpedoes to have time to arm. Morton ordered full speed and full right rudder. The Wahoo spun around and put some distance between itself and the anticipated track of the enemy. As they reached a new firing position, Morton slowed the boat and O'Kane took the scope. The convoy was really coming on now—no time for a second look.

The order was given and two torpedoes were sent toward the lead ship—one to the mainmast, and one to the foremast. They repeated the procedure and fired two more at the second ship as the first two scored hits. This second salvo scored one hit.

Through the scope, O'Kane saw the first ship listing to one side and sinking. Confused by the excitement, he took the long way around to find the second ship. As he was turning, a third ship was spotted heading right for them! Morton decided to shoot down-the-throat again, but as soon as he said the word shoot, the firing officer hit the plunger and fired a torpedo in error. Seeing this shot, the ship started to turn away. This gave O'Kane his first good look at it. It turned out to be a big one, a troop carrier! The troop ship captain made a big mistake by turning away from the sub. Now it presented a much bigger target of which O'Kane and Morton quickly took advantage. When the range was called out at 1200 yards and the angle-on-the-bow was 70 degrees port, two more torpedoes were fired.

The crew of the Wahoo then turned its attention back to the second freighter, which had been hit once. It was still under power, at six knots, and was headed straight for the sub. It was time for another down-the-throat shot. Just before firing, they were gladdened by two explosions that could only have been the two fish headed for the troop ship. Two more torpedoes were now ready and immediately heading for the freighter. The first proved to be a dud but the second hit and exploded. All in the conning tower were surprised to see the freighter shake it off and keep on coming!

There was nothing to do now but go deep. They sat quietly at 100 feet, letting the soundman sort out the ships left on the surface. After a short break, they headed back up, ready to shoot. Back at the periscope depth, they saw the freighter heading away and the troop ship dead in the water. It would be the next victim. They lined the ship up and fired. The first shot was another dud, but the second did the job.

Torpedo Attack # 3

The heading of the damaged freighter and another ship were plotted for pursuit. After putting a charge on the Wahoo's batteries, all engines went online as Morton began a long chase and end-around maneuver. Keeping the ships just below the horizon, Morton conned the ship to a position ahead of the group. He then ordered her down for a submerged approach and attack. The second undamaged ship was a tanker, which would be the first target.

The submerged approach brought Wahoo to a good firing position, and quickly, three fish were headed toward the tanker. Immediately, Morton ordered full speed and full rudder as he swung the sub around to bring the stern tubes to bear. As the Wahoo was turning, one torpedo hit the tanker, and , with a flash, started a fire—but she wasn't about to sink yet. Now they had four torpedoes left to sink two damaged ships.

Getting a good shot on the damaged freighter was a problem. It seemed that no matter how he approached, the sub was spotted and the ship took evasive action. After a while, Morton ordered all ahead back and they went back after the smoking tanker, backwards. Two shots were fired and they were rewarded with a hit. That should do it, Morton decided, ordering all ahead full. Once more they pursued the sturdy freighter. A surface approach was foiled by gunfire from the freighter and Wahoo went deep.

After a short while they surfaced again, moved ahead of the freighter, and waited. As the ship moved into firing position, a destroyer appeared on the horizon. They would have one last shot. Keeping the stern pointed at the target as it approached, Morton gave the order and the last two torpedoes were fired. All fingers were crossed—they wanted a sinking, not merely damage.

After a long three-minute run, both fish hit; finally, the tough Arizona Maru-class freighter began to sink. The Wahoo headed for Pearl Harbor, flying a broom tied to the mast to indicate a clean sweep. Morton radioed his attack report and received the now famous reply from Admiral Halsey, "Your picture is on the piano!"

On the way back to Pearl, O'Kane had the unusual experience of two birthdays when they crossed the International Date Line and gained another 2 February 1943. This was the best patrol of the war so far and the Wahoo was awarded a Presidential Unit Citation.

10 USS Wahoo: 4th Patrol

The Wahoo's successful third patrol was the shortest on record at that time—only 24 days. So after an equally short rest of eight days, they were off to sea again. Their reward for such a successful patrol was a trip into Empire waters, heading to Midway and on to the East China and Yellow seas.

After an uneventful Pacific crossing, the Wahoo and crew passed through the Colnett Strait and into the East China Sea in the cover of darkness on 11 March 1943. The Colnett Strait is a major passageway between Japan's large Kyushu Island and a group of smaller islands to the south, known collectively as the Ryukyu Islands. Morton then headed north to the Formosa-Nagasaki shipping lanes. Several days of submerged patrolling during the day and on the surface at night didn't produce a single contact.

Torpedo Attack # 1

Finally, on 13 March, near the large island Saishu To, the call of "smoke on the horizon" sent the crew to battle stations. A small freighter slowly came into view and the captain determined that it was worth one torpedo. The Wahoo was sitting almost directly on her track, so the captain conned the ship slightly out of her path and waited.

One torpedo in the aft torpedo room was readied. The target's estimated speed was 12 knots, and when she presented a favorable angle, O'Kane gave the order to fire. The shot broached the surface and then headed toward the target, finally passing in front of it. The freighter turned out to be smaller than they originally thought, leading to an overestimation of her speed, which was probably closer to 10 knots.

The crew learned from this mistake and vowed not to repeat it. At least the freighter hadn't seen the errant shot, so the sub's presence in the area was still unknown.

Richard O'Kane (left) and Commander Dudley "Mush" Morton on the bridge of the Wahoo.

Torpedo Attack # 2

Another uneventful day passed and the Wahoo headed north to the Yellow Sea. Early on the morning of 19 March, the Bells of Saint Mary's sent the crew to battle stations again. The sub raced to gain a position ahead of the large freighter coming into view, and when it reached a position 750 yards off her track, the captain ordered the sub to submerge. He waited until the ship was headed slightly away from the sub—on a 120-degree angle—to fire. This aspect would allow for maximum enemy evasive maneuvers and still ensure a hit.

The order to fire was given and, quickly, a single torpedo was on its way. After a short 49-second run, there was a huge explosion. This was the first hit with the new Torpex explosive head, and it was quite impressive. The ship's stern was totally blown away; two minutes and 26 seconds later, what was left of the ship sank.

Torpedo Attack # 3

Later on the morning of 19 March, as the captain finished breakfast, the call came again—another freighter was sighted. The ship had already pulled even with the sub, so a long chase to firing position was in store. By 0900 their submerged chase brought them into firing position at a range of 2000 yards.

The captain waited for the 120-degree track again and then gave O'Kane the go-ahead to fire. Two torpedoes hit the freighter—in the bow and amidships, but she didn't appear ready to sink.

Two more fish were fired, but the skillful Japanese captain managed to avoid them both. With low batteries, the sub couldn't continue the chase submerged and it would have been foolish to surface and face the ship's large guns. So, when the Japanese started firing at the periscope, Morton decided to head for deep water and clear the area.

Torpedo Attack # 4

The evening of 21 March found the Wahoo just off the Korean shore, waiting for ships along a logical shipping lane. As the off-duty officers were settling in for the night, a call from the Officer of the Deck (OOD) brought them running.

A ship had been spotted. There seemed to be plenty of time to move to a firing position. The initial range was 7000 yards. During the setup, the ship made a zig in the Wahoo's direction that made the approach even better. The ship was at least 7000 tons, probably a passenger freighter. Again, they waited as the ship passed perpendicular to them. When the ship was at the 120-degree position, Wahoo fired. Three torpedoes were on their way, one in the stern, one in the bow, and one in the middle. The first missed behind, the second missed in front, but the third hit right in the middle. The ship started down almost immediately. Four and a half minutes later, she was gone.

Torpedo Attack # 5

Shortly after dawn on 21 March, another ship came over the horizon. Little maneuvering was necessary as he moved toward them. It was a perfect setup—all they had to do was wait.

As the target passed in front of the Wahoo, three torpedoes were sent on their way from the after torpedo room. The run was short; it only took 52 seconds to cross the 800 yards. Two solid hits followed and the members of the crew took turns watching as the ship slid beneath the flat sea. A battle surface was immediately ordered and shortly thereafter, swimmers were sent into the flotsam to look for codebooks and maps. A number of books were retrieved along with numerous souvenirs for the crew, which included two large flags of the steamship line and a life preserver bearing the ship's name, Nitu Maru.

Torpedo Attack # 6

Just before dawn on 23 March, radar packed up a ship; the Wahoo was patrolling the western side of the Yellow Sea near the entrance to the Gulf of Po Hai. A quick surface run put the Wahoo ahead of her and on her track—they would submerge and attack at dawn. O'Kane took the scope and watched the ship approach: The range closed to 2000 yards; the angle-on-the-bow was 88 degrees. Another perfect setup.

One torpedo was fired, hitting right under the ship's stack, raising a large black cloud as it was carrying coal. With such a heavy load, it started for the bottom immediately. The Wahoo was definitely on a roll.

Torpedo Attack # 7

On the evening of 24 March, the crew was settling in to watch the evening movie when the bells rang to bring them to battle stations. A large tanker was headed straight for them.

A stern shot seemed appropriate. Morton conned the boat to a favorable position and O'Kane took the TBT (Target Bearing Transmitter) on the bridge. At 1700 yards, three torpedoes were on their way. Two exploded prematurely 18 seconds later, rocking the Wahoo, but not the enemy. The third was knocked off course. One more torpedo was fired, but the ship had changed course by then and it missed also.

The tracking team and Morton decided that the tanker must be headed for the port in Dairen. If the sub surfaced and "poured it on," it could beat her there. An hour or so running at flank speed on the surface put the Wahoo in good position ahead of the target and still four miles from the port. The tanker was silhouetted in the rising moon so they could use the scope and attack submerged.

This close to port, the tanker's captain was obviously feeling safe: He brought the ship straight down the track and made a perfect target. O'Kane lined it up and Morton ordered three shots. The first two missed for and aft, but again, the third struck right in the middle—the best place to hit a tanker. They watched in the conning tower as the Syoyo Maru, 7500 tons, sank be the stern. Morton ordered the Wahoo to the surface to leave the area and the crew returned to watching their movie.

Torpedo Attack # 8

Later on the night of 24 March, the fire control party was quietly called to the bridge. Another ship had wandered into Wahoo territory and conditions were good with enough moon for tracking and enough time before dawn to obtain a good position.

Finally in position just before 0400—and they had an excellent position 10,0000 yards ahead of the enemy and 1000 yards off her track—'the Wahoo submerged and the crew was called to battle stations.

As the ship pulled broadside to the sub, two torpedoes were fired. The first fish exploded before it reached the target but the second hit with a loud explosion. It was a solid hit, but the freighter just kept going. Morton ordered, "Battle surface, gun!" A quick 12 minutes later, the Wahoo was on the surface and pumping shells into the freighter.

The captain's attention was then drawn away by the reported sighting of another ship. Afraid that it might be a warship, he ordered cease-fire and turned to investigate. The sighting turned out to be a small tanker apparently approaching to determine the source of smoke. By this time, the freighter was full of holes, on fire, listing, and sinking. The gun crew took a short rest while Morton conned the Wahoo toward the small tanker. A running gun battle gave the gun crew another good workout, and in the end, they set the tanker ablaze. As the sub left the area on the surface, the crew on deck watched both ships sink.

Torpedo Attack # 9

With only two torpedoes left, the Wahoo spent the next several days in search of shipping in the Yellow Sea and back into the East China Sea. Finally, in the early morning darkness of 30 March, the crew spotted a ship. Morton conned the boat patiently for another submerged dawn attack. As the sun began to rise in the east, the bell sounded, sending the Wahoo's crew to battle stations for the last time of the patrol. With its last two torpedoes, the Wahoo sent this medium-sized freighter to the bottom.

Morton put the boat on the surface and headed back through the Colnett Strait toward home.

11 USS Wahoo: 7th Patrol

The Wahoo's sixth patrol turned out to be a nightmare for Commander Morton: The crew had driven deep into the Sea of Japan, found numerous targets, and then came away with no success stories. The problem was the MK 14 torpedo. Time after time, Morton conned the boat to a good firing position and fired perfect shots only to be greeted by a thud at impact and no explosion. After attacks on nine ships with no detonations, Morton wisely decided that it was futile to keep shooting bad torpedoes and that it would be better to take them back to Pearl Harbor where the failures could be investigated.

Morton's stay at Pearl was short, and he demanded to be allowed to return to the Sea of Japan, this time with "live fish." His request was granted and in early September 1943, the Wahoo and the USS Sawfish left Pearl for Empire waters, both secretly armed with new MK 18 torpedoes. The Wahoo had a full load of 24; the Sawfish carried a load half MK 14 and half MK 18.

What actually happened aboard the Wahoo during this last patrol will never be known. Numerous writers have speculated as to her fate, but the most convincing account was written by one of the men who knew the boat and its skipper best—Richard O'Kane. By this time, O' Kane had left the Wahoo to assume his own command, but his interest and love for the Wahoo led him to investigate her fate after the war. His account was based on tracking reports by the Japanese Navy, Japanese newspaper accounts of ships lost, his knowledge of Commander Morton, and his own tragic personal experience with the MK 18 torpedo.

Torpedo Attack # 1

The Wahoo entered the Sea of Japan again through the La Perouse Strait; the night transit was uneventful. After careful patrolling down the coast, the crew sighted a group of ships headed their way. Crew members went to battle stations for the first time in that patrol, confident in Morton's ability to sink enemy ships. A medium freighter pulled into view and the tracking party went to work.

A steady approach was made and two torpedoes were fired from close range. The wait during the run must have seemed endless: The electric MK 18 traveled only half as fast as the MK 14, but left no wake to point a finger at the firing sub. The wait did end eventually with the impact and explosion of both torpedoes; the freighter was completely blown up. Torpedo confidence regained, Morton cleared the area. He often used this hit-and-run tactic, not staying in one pace long enough to let the anti-submarine ships close in.

Torpedo Attack # 2

Five days later, another ship showed up on the SJ (surface) radar and the crew started tracking. With sundown just ahead, there wasn't enough time for a periscope attack, but they did get a good look at her—a small cargo ship. The Wahoo surfaced and waited; the target was coming right down the track toward them. Two shots were fired, resulting in a hit, and the target broke in two and sank. The Wahoo was back in business.

Torpedo Attack # 3

Morton had made a prewar trip into these waters and he knew he should move the sub to a position in a heavily used traveling lane across the southern part of the sea. On 5 October, escorts were sighted. The Wahoo approached slowly and made contact with a large ship. Easily slipping past the escorts, the captain took up a position off the target track and set up for a straight bow shot. From only 950 yards, they opened fire with four torpedoes spread to hit along the ship's length. They all hit and exploded, ripping the side out of the large troop transport.

Flooded totally on one side, the transport rolled over and sank. This sinking was reported in the Japanese press and could only have been attributed to the Wahoo. A brief depth charge attack followed, but it was quickly put astern as the Wahoo once again moved out of a hot area before a massive anti-submarine operation could be mounted.

Three ships down so early in the patrol must have lifted the crew's spirits after the disappointing 6th patrol. The mood stayed high as another ship appeared on the SJ; battle stations were called, but most of the stations were already manned.

Again, the Wahoo had a good set up, and tubes both fore and aft were made ready in case of a wild last-minute zig. None came. Two fish were fired form the stern tubes, again resulting in hits. The Wahoo followed its familiar pattern: Dive, clear the area, and cheer.

Torpedo Attack # 4

Weather turned bad as the Wahoo approached the Tsugaru Strait area, but the SJ burned through the muck to spot a ship moving down a track toward them. Morton moved on the ship's tack; then, keeping the stern pointed at the ship to show only a minimum angle, he fired three torpedoes at the medium-sized freighter. It was immediately obvious that something was wrong. One of the torpedoes made a wide zig to the side, possible hitting the bow on the way out of the tube, and started to circle.

Emergency power was called, but it wasn't enough. The torpedo came all the way around and struck the Wahoo, flooding several departments. She was damaged, but not down for the count. If at all possible, Morton would have headed for home to return the MK 18s for investigation. Unable to dive, she tried to make through the La Perouse Strait on the surface under overcast skies. The sub was spotted by a shore artillery battery and fired upon. Left with no choice but to dive, Commander Morton blew the tanks and headed down, but those on the shore had called for air attacks and arrived shortly.

Oil leaking from ruptured fuel tanks was easily spotted by the bombers and they closed in for the kill. Numerous small bombs reportedly were dropped on this oil slick, followed by several large depth charges that brought up a large piece of bright metal identified as a propeller. This was most likely the end of the Wahoo.

It's unfortunate that Morton didn't return with the MK 18s; if he had, he would surely have prevented similar disasters. After the war, the MK 18 was tested, and its tendency to make circular runs was verified.

Commander "Mush" Morton was a true pioneer in submarine tactics. This captain and his ship were greatly missed by the Pacific sub forces. His legacy was the men he trained, such as Dick O'Kane. O'Kane went on to do great things with his own command, the USS Tang. He was awarded the Congressional Medal of Honor by President Truman in March 1946.

12   USS Trigger: 6th Patrol

The 6th patrol of the USS Trigger was short in duration but long in achievement. The entire patrol was accomplished in the month of September 1943. It was a lesson in dogged determination as the captain and crew launched on a large convoy and made prepared attacks until they had damaged or sunk almost the entire convoy.

They set sail from Pearl Harbor on 1 September 1943, headed for their patrol area in the East China Sea.

Torpedo Attack # 1

More than half the month passed before the crew of the Trigger had a chance to make a real approach on a target, the first of which came on the afternoon of 17 September as a five-ship convoy was sighted moving at high speed. They opened up the engines and made an attempt to gain a firing position ahead of the group but were finally forced to admit that they were not going to catch it. By 1745, they had lost contact with the convoy.

The sub slowed to normal patrol speed, an the crew was about to settle in for another night when the lookouts spotted two ships running on an opposite course from their own. The captain allowed the two large freighters to pass by and prepared to surface and attack after dark.

Darkness fell with authority that night—visibility was almost nil. The Trigger approached quietly on the surface and fired four torpedoes at the largest ship from 1100 yards the captain and crew were stunned to see two hits—both of which were duds!

The target was now alerted to the sub's presence, so the captain ordered the Trigger to submerge for a reload as the Japanese sailors opened fire with deck guns. Captain Dornin took the boat around to the other side of the ship and came up to fire again. The Trigger moved in to 1000 yards and fired four torpedoes. Two hits were seen, and the shocks from the explosions were felt through out the submarine. The target ship was in trouble with the first hit; after the second, it quickly sank.

With this warm-up successfully under their belts, the crew went looking for a serious convoy and found it on 21 September.

Torpedo Attack # 2

In the later afternoon, masts were sighted on the horizon; the Trigger approached at high speed. A convoy was contacted consisting of one large tanker, two small tankers, and three medium-sized freighters; it had air coverage but no escorts.

After dark, the Trigger surfaced and chased the group. Once abeam of the tanker column, the captain turned the sub to make a surface attack. As the range closed, he fired three torpedoes at the barge tanker from 21,600 yards and then turned the sub again and fired three more at a second tanker.

One torpedo hit toward the stern of the first tanker and flames shot 500 feet into the air. A second torpedo hit her amidships but nothing could add to the holocaust already taking place. The second tanker took a hit amid ships and began to burn also; after being hit, she turned hard away from the Trigger.

One shot that missed hit a tanker in the next column and broke it in two; this tanker sank immediately. The burning tankers completely lit the area so all the ships, as well as the sub, were plainly visible. The remaining ships all opened on the sub, but their aim wasn't true and the shots missed the Trigger by the a comfortable margin. One tanker did get the captain's attention, however, when it turned and rushed toward the sub firing its bow gun.

Captain Dornin turned the sub and headed away from the oncoming tanker; it seemed to take forever to build up speed as the tanker grew larger and larger. As the sub turned, it sent three torpedoes after the tanker, but all missed. Once the sub steadied her course, the captain fired one torpedo down-the-throat and score a hit as he pulled away.

By this time, shells from the ships' guns began to close in, so Captain Dornin ordered the Trigger to dive in order to sort things out. There was momentary confusion in the conning tower as the captain fell into the periscope well, but he was able to catch himself by the elbows. He called to the quartermaster just in time to stop him from lowering the scope.

When several violent explosions were heard, the captain ordered the sub to periscope depth to take a look around; Tanker number 1 and tanker number 2 were both stopped and burning; tanker number 3 was down by the bow; one of the freighters had sunk. Trigger surfaced and pursued a freighter that was trying to run to the north. They approached on the surface and fired the last two bow torpedoes, resulting in two hits. The target started sinking immediately.

The freighter the Trigger had just attacked was down a little in the bow but now ready to sink; the captain ordered the sub to close in so he could finish off the ship. Two stern torpedoes were fired at the stationary target from 2200 yards, but nothing happened—there must have been at least one dud. The ship was now able to get underway again and was getting very close with the deck gun, so Dornin took the Trigger down, and they made several approaches before they could get a shot with the stern tubes. The last two torpedoes were fired from a perfect setup—a 90-degree target angle and a range of only 1000 yards. Screams and curses filled the boat as both turned out to be duds. The captain considered a battle surface and gun action, but the old three-inch gun had never fired more than five consecutive rounds in its history without jamming, so the idea was dropped.

All torpedoes expended, the crew of the Trigger pointed their bow toward Midway.

13   USS Seahorse 2nd Patrol

One of the most consistent boats of the war was the Seahorse, who turned in a string of very successful patrols. The first of these was her 2nd patrol, the first under Commander Slade D. Cutter. Commander Cutter and crew departed Midway on 20 October 1943 to patrol south of the Empire in the East China Sea.

The Seahorse had been at sea for only nine days when it approached a small trawler and sank it with the deck gun. The scene was repeated the next day and this time, valuable charts were recovered as well as fresh fish for supper.

Torpedo Attack #1

A few hours after the gun action, a large 17-ship convoy was sighted. Through the night, the skipper tried to obtain a good firing position. At about 0300, the Seahorse was submerged and ready to fire; then, one of the escorts turned and the entire setup was ruined as the captain had to take the sub deep to avoid being rammed in the darkness.

Back on the surface a little later, he began yet another end-around maneuver. This time as he approached, he saw an explosion toward the end of the convoy—another US. sub was making an attack! Rather than being upset over having to share his quarry, Cutter felt the action might drive some of the ships his way. It was extremely dark, and so the captain decided to remain on the surface for the attack.

Several dark shapes appeared off the bow, and he closed in for an attack. Three torpedoes were fired at a small freighter, resulting in hits. The freighter broke up and sank. The captain ordered full speed and headed away from the convoy to set up again.

Torpedo Attack # 2

Four hours later, the sub returned to the surface. This time, a large tanker and a medium-sized freighter were the targets. Three fish were fired at each and each ship took too hits. With an escort now on his tail, Cutter ordered flank speed and the sub pulled away.

After that, things were slow for "the Horse" for a while, and for several days, the crew was unable to find any enemy shipping.

Torpedo Attack # 3

On 22 November, the Seahorse's luck finally changed: A convoy of two freighters and three escorts steamed over the horizon.

An approach was made, but the escorts were very active and constantly in the way. After several attempts, a firing position was reached and four torpedoes were fired at the lead freighter. Two hit and she went down in several pieces. Before the sub could fire at the second target, an escort forced her deep and by the time she got back to the surface, the Seahorse had lost contact with the other ship.

Torpedo Attack # 4

At dusk on 27 November, the gong once again sounded to bring the crew to battle stations.

A heavily loaded freighter and two large tankers came into view, along with three escorts riding herd. Again, several surface approaches were foiled by the escorts and changes in direction. The group appeared to be heading for the Tsushima Straits, which were believed to be mined. If they made it that far, Cutter knew he couldn't follow—he had to catch them before they got there.

He poured on the fuel, drew as close as he dared, and fired four torpedoes at one of the tankers. The range was extreme. He immediately turned to try a stern shot, but the range was now too great. He maneuvered again to try one more shot and was welcomed by two torpedo hits from the first salvo.

The tanker broke in two and each part sank separately. Dodging an escort, Commander Cutter fired four more fish at the second tanker, resulting in two more hits. The bridge crew watched for several seconds as flames slowly appeared from the tanker. At first, it didn't seem badly damaged, but then they were all shocked by an enormous explosion. Flames shot 3500 feet into the air and parts of the ship flew huge distances in all directions. An escort made a halfhearted attempt to attack the Seahorse, but it, too, may have been damaged by the explosion.

Now low on fuel, the submarine started back to Midway.

Torpedo Attack #5

While heading home, the Seahorse happened upon a small, fast-moving convoy. Having torpedoes left only in the stern tubes, the approach was very difficult. Each time the Seahorse pulled ahead of the convoy, it had taken a turn and wasn't where the sub thought it would be.

Finally, everything came together at once: The Seahorse fired four stern torpedoes and the entire convoy began firing deck guns at the Seahorse. In the resulting pandemonium, no one could say for sure whether any of the torpedoes hit. The captain was almost certain he had hit something, but to his credit, he didn't claim damage.

He did claim to sink seven ships on the Seahorse's 2nd patrol, but his official total was changed after the war to show five ships sunk for a very respectable total tonnage of 27,500.

Slade Cutter had mastered the night surface approach and used it well on this patrol. It was a very effective maneuver when executed properly.

14   USS Seahorse 3rd Patrol

After a quick fueling at Midway, the Seahorse was off to Pearl Harbor for a refit and training. On 6 January 1944, she sailed from Pearl Harbor on her 3rd war patrol to sweep the seas in the area of the Palau Islands.

Torpedo Attack #1

While Seahorse was underway on the morning of 16 January, the watch spotted a freighter and four escorts. Hoping to use some of the stern torpedoes early, Captain Cutter maneuvered the boat to a good firing position, but the target zigged away at the last minute.

With all our escorts on his side of the ship, Cutter decided to hold fire and circle out for a surface end-around. By 1607, after avoiding a depth charge attack launched by one of the escorts, Seahorse was on the surface and running at flank speed. At 2009, they were far enough ahead of the group to turn and start the approach. Heading in as close as possible, they fired four torpedoes at the freighter, three solid hits were seen. The first two set the target ablaze and the third blew off her stern.

The next several days were spent correcting damage caused by depth charges. The captain's questions regarding how the escort managed to keep contact with them were answered when the sub surfaced—they spotted a large oil slick on the water, where an oil filler cap had come loose. Once the cap was tightened, the oil slick disappeared.

Torpedo Attack #2

On 19 January, they approached Fais Island for reconnaissance. After entering the area, the Seahorse contacted two enemy cargo ships with three escorts on 21 January. The captain tracked the ships all day and then as dusk drew near, he made a surface approach and fired three torpedoes at one of the freighters.

Two hits were scored on the target, and one torpedo hit a ship behind the target. "The Japanese were no more surprised (by the third hit) than we were," noted Cutter. Both ships stopped and opened fire in every direction while the escorts randomly dropped charges. The Seahorse followed at a safe distance and watched as the first ship sank bow first. Two more shots were fired at the second ship, but both missed. The fire team huddled, and after recalculating the numbers, fired two more with the same results. Again they huddled and decided that the Target Bearing Transmitter must be "out of whack." A third salvo was fired, and this time, both torpedoes were dead on. Down went the target.

Torpedo Attack #3

By 29 January, the Seahorse had moved down to Palau Island and contacted three freighters and five escorts coming by the island. Several attempts to close on the surface in the dark were foiled by escorts continually moving between the sub and its targets.

Realizing that this was not going to work, Commander Cutter raced the sub ahead for a submerged approach. At dawn, the convoy changed course and once again left the Seahorse out in the cold. She tracked the convoy all day and surfaced again at dusk and moved in to attack. Again the escorts frustrated the captain but he stayed with the attack. Finally, at 0130, the freighters made a mistake. They made a radical zig that put the escorts out of position. It was a race to the firing point and the Seahorse was much faster than the escorts. She moved in and fired three torpedoes, resulting in three hits. The target sank as she withdrew.

Torpedo Attack # 4

At dawn, the sub lost contact with the convoy but managed to maintain a bearing on it by listening to the destroyer's sonar "pinging." By mid-afternoon, the convoy split. After dark, the Seahorse surfaced again to continue the hunt. She regained radar contact, and shortly after midnight, finally fired four torpedoes at a large freighter. And missed. Another two shots also missed. The torpedoes couldn't hit the freighter because of its defensive zig-zag pattern.

Torpedo Attack #5

Now Cutter had only two shots remaining, and he wanted to make them count. At 0300, he started a submerged approach and closed to within 800 yards of the target. As soon as the last two tubes were cleared, the Seahorse headed deep to avoid three escorts close at hand. Torpedo hits were mixed with the sound of depth charges for the next several minutes. Later, Commander Cutter surfaced to find that he had hit the target. He watched as it sank, framed by burning gasoline.

All out of torpedoes, the Seahorse headed back to Pearl with five new victims for her battle flag.

15   USS Seashorse 4th Patrol

With two very successful patrols now under his belt with the Seahorse, Slade Cutter sailed confidently from Pearl on 16 March 1944. His destination was the Mariana Islands—he wanted to make three excellent patrols in a row.

After avoiding another submarine and several aircraft attacks, they started to patrol on 28 March.

Torpedo Attack #1

Just off Tinian Island on 4 April, the Seahorse came into contact with her first convoy of the patrol. Seahorse followed the convoy until it slipped into the harbor, preventing an approach.

Cutter stayed in the area for a few days hoping to catch a group coming out the harbor. His persistence was rewarded on 7 April as the watch sighted a five-ship convoy—three freighters and two escorts. Around 0100 the next morning, he submerged well ahead of the convoy and slipped past the escorts to a good firing position. The ships then made a turn to the right and Cutter decided to fire rather than wait for a better setup

Three torpedoes were fired at the first target at a range of 1200 yards, with only showing a 30-degree angle on the bow. As the second target was about to be overlapped by the first, they fired three shots at it. The second target was at a range of 220 yards with a somewhat better angle on the bow of 50 degrees.

The first target took all three hits with a tremendous explosion. The captain turned the periscope around to look for escorts, and by the time he turned back to the target, it was gone. The second ship also took a hit and was on fire but apparently on an even keel.

The escorts closed in and the crew of the Seahorse waited out the barrage of 28 depth charges. The escorts kept them in shallow water for quite awhile before they could break contact and move out to sea. After quickly charging the batteries, Commander Cutter tried to locate the second ship again to finish the job, but when the sub returned to the scene, all that was left was a large oil slick.

Torpedo Attack #2

Cutter's luck held and 9 April found him on the trail of yet another good-sized convoy. With the periscope fogging badly, it was hard for him to determine the exact makeup of the group, but there were at least 15 or 20 ships.

The largest freighter moved to the opposite side of the group and out of range, but a quite respectable one moved into a position it would later regret. With an excellent setup of 1800 yards and 85 degree angle on the bow, the Seahorse fired a four-torpedo spread, but just as the third torpedo was fired, the ships made a sharp turn. All four shots missed. Undaunted, Cutter set up and fired two more with the new course information and scored two quick hits.

He had several tense moments then: One of the first torpedoes circled back toward him and ran in rings for quite a while. The escorts closed in for a harmless counterattack and the crew of the sub listened to surface explosions and breaking up noises from their target.

Back at periscope depth somewhat later, Cutter was discouraged to see the target still afloat. He surfaced and cleared the area to get a quick battery charge. The Seahorse eluded two destroyers and closed in on the scene of the earlier attack. After a long night of trying to get back to the damaged ship, they were glad to find only floating debris in the area. The ship had sunk during the night, and wreckage was strewn all the way to the horizon. It's possible that another ship was hit and sunk as well.

The Seahorse and crew spent several days playing tag with a group of destroyers and aircraft sent out from Guam.

Torpedo Attack #3

Cutter took the boat over to Saipan for a while, hoping to let things cool off in the area. While the crew tried to judge the depth of the water west of Saipan, a Japanese submarine was sighted on the surface at 210 degrees. Because of the amount of time he had spent in the area earlier in the patrol, Cutter was confident as he approached the other boat submerged.

Having tracked the sub for long enough to make out its base course and zig-zag pattern, he moved in to attack. Seahorse slowed to let the sub pass. When its range was 1600 yards, it presented a good 85-degree angle on the bow. Two torpedoes were fired: One very loud hit was heard and Captain Cutter believed the enemy sub blew up.

Torpedo Attack #4

At breakfast time on 26 April, another convoy was spotted, and the crew went to battle stations. The convoy was making slow speed, so it was decided to secure from battle stations and track the group all day; then they would attack at night.

After dark, the Seahorse took up a position dead ahead of the convoy and waited for it to approach. When contact was again made, the group was heading straight for the sub. Cutter turned the boat toward the convoy. Although he hadn't reached a good firing position, it appeared that one of the escorts had spotted them, so Cutter took the boat around to use the stern tubes. Four torpedoes were fired. Even though the angle on the bow was a narrow 38 degrees, three hits were observed through the periscope and the target sank quietly by the stern. The escort counterattack was "hardly worth the name." A few charges were dropped but none came close.

There wasn't enough time for another attack that night, and since the Seahorse had orders for lifeguard duty shortly, Commander Cutter broke contact with the convoy and headed toward his next station.

When lifeguard duty was completed, she headed to Brisbane for a well-deserved rest. The Seahorse was out of torpedoes.

16 USS Bowfin 2nd Patrol

Admiral Christie, the commander of all U.S. submarines based in Australia, was so pleased with the first patrol of the Bowfin that he promoted its skipper, Commander Willingham, to head a submarine division. Christie's choice for replacement was Lt. Commander Walter Thomas Griffith, recently the XO (Executive Officer) aboard the USS Gar.

On it's first voyage, the Bowfin had formed an impromptu wolf pack with the Billfish with very good results. Impressed by their performance, Christie assigned the two to work together again. On 1 November 1943, after an appropriate period of leave and a week of get-acquainted drill and training, the Bowfin set out of Freemantle,

Australia on its second patrol of the war. After a quick stop at Exmouth Gulf (a forward fuel station) to top off its tanks, Griffith headed toward Lombok Strait to pass into the Java Sea and Japanese-controlled territory. During this period, Griffith was irritated to notice that an oil slick was present after every morning trim dive. He attributed this to overfilling the tanks at Exmouth. After several days of travel, the fuel level was down but the slick appeared again, and so the crew spend a hard day's work plugging and tightening connections. This seemed to cure the problem, but the cruise was off to a rocky start.

On the morning of 9 November, lookouts spotted a schooner, but seconds later, the hunter became the hunted as a Japanese bomber came out of the clouds and forced the Bowfin to crash dive. The plane loitered around for 20 minutes before giving up and heading away. When the boat surfaced, it was faced with not one, but five schooners under sail. Griffith ordered battle-stations-gun and the crew quickly sank three of the ships with the four-inch gun. The craft sank so uncommonly fast that the commander justified the attack by stating that they must have been carrying something heavy. The crew, however, felt the attack was unwarranted since women and children were aboard.

Another patrol plane forced the Bowfin to break off the attack. The plane circled overhead long enough for the two remaining ships to escape, obviously protecting them. Even so, Griffith would later state that he regretted the attack.

The sub surfaced again later in the afternoon only to be driven deep immediately by another bomb-carrying patrol plane. Griffith decided they were too close to shore and headed out to deeper waters toward Balikpapan and the Celebes Sea. Later that evening, they sank another schooner with the deck gun.

Torpedo Attack #1

The Celebes Sea area was reputed to be a heavy Japanese shipping zone, and Griffith was discouraged after several days. The only things sighted had been Japanese planes. His luck finally changed around 1700 on 11 November when lookouts spotted smoke on the horizon—a convoy. The ships were zig-zagging and hard to keep up with, so Griffith decided they must be headed for the Sibutu Channel and he set out to beat them there.

Around 1930, two ships steamed into sight in the moonlight. The book identified them as coastal tankers, and they were traveling without an escort. Griffith examined the situation and decided that he should attack from the mouth of the bay to prevent either ship from getting away. By 2100, the Bowfin was in position, and by 2130, the targets were close enough to tell that they weren't armed. A surface gun attack would be safe. At 2150, the Bowfin opened fire, and shortly afterward, both targets were in flames. Being so close to the shore again made Griffith nervous, so he quickly left the area and headed north at full speed.

Several days of patrolling Mindanao and the Philippines were uneventful, and on 14 November, the Bowfin headed into the South China Sea in a storm to try and meet with the Billfish. After several missed connections, the two subs eventually found each other, exchanged information, and parted again. The Bowfin headed on toward the Indochina coast, and on 25 November, made land fall. Due to the poor quality of his maps of the area, Griffith wasn't certain exactly where he was, and on several occasions, he barely managed to keep from running aground in the storm that plagued his boat for days.

Torpedo Attack #2

Around 0200 on 26 November, a dark shape suddenly appeared on a collision course. Several minutes later, when the collision almost happened again, Griffith realized that he had wandered into the middle of a Japanese convoy! A radar sweep showed five ships and an escort craft.

Griffith lined the submarine up for an attack on the two largest ships. AT 0351, he fired three torpedoes at the first one. As he started setting up for the second ship, two of the three torpedoes hit the first ship and stopped it dead in the water.

He managed to get off one torpedo at the second target before having to change course and reverse engines to avoid a collision with the first ship. The shot ran true and the second ship took its first hit. He swung the stern around hoping to take care of the first ship before the escort arrived. One of the stern torpedo tube doors jammed, so three shots were fired: One hit the first ship and one was lucky hit on the second ship. With both targets in bad shape and all tubes empty, the Bowfin headed away from the area to reload.

By 0530, the Bowfin was ready to head back in at full speed. On the way back to the area of the attack, the sub almost ran head-on into the hull of one of the tankers hit earlier, now sinking rapidly. Finding only an oil slick at the scene of the battle, the captain headed after the convoy and tried to contact the Billfish.

Torpedo Attack #3

Around 0830, the watch spotted a steamer of approximately 5000 tons. After a two-hour chase and maneuver period, Griffith fired four torpedoes and was rewarded with four hits. The ship went under in less than two minutes.

Torpedo Attack #4

At 0200 on 28 November, the Bill fish contacted the Bowfin about a convoy seen headed their way. Aided with this information, Griffith managed to get the Bowfin ahead of the convoy and into attack position in only an hour. The convoy consisted of five large ships and several smaller escorts. Griffith quietly slipped between the escorts and the ships, and at 0314, he opened fire.

Six torpedoes from the bow tubes left two of the largest ships sinking in a matter of minutes. The captain of the third ship had other ideas however; he turned toward the Bowfin intent on ramming, and opened fire with his five-inch deck gun.

Griffith swung the stern of the sub toward the convoy hoping to finish off the second ship now wallowing deep in the water, but the third ship was closing fast. As it came within 500 yards, one of the five-inch shells found its mark on the rear of the sub. A quick glance at the second ship showed that it should be going under on its own shortly, so angered by the shell hit, Griffith and his crew turned their attention to the third ship, which was getting uncomfortably close. With this ship only 300 yards away and coming on like a locomotive, the Bowfin fired two stern torpedoes. Both hit home. The Japanese ship broke in half and sank by the middle.

Surprisingly, the escorts hadn't come after the Bowfin but had concentrated on moving the rest of the convoy away. Griffith gave chase on the surface, afraid to dive because he was unsure of the damaged caused to the pressure hull by the gun hit. By 0340, he caught up with the convoy again and fired his last two torpedoes. Both missed. Griffith continued to track the group and directed the Billfish on an intercept course. When the Billfish made contact with the convoy, Griffith moved the Bowfin away from the area to check the damage.

An inspection showed that a number of pipes and induction lines had been broken, but the pressure hull was intact. Repairs were made as best they could be. The boat still took on water when submerged, but the pumps were able to handle it, so with all torpedoes expended, the Bowfin turned and headed for home.

Along the way on 2 December, back in the Makassar Strait, they spotted and sank another yacht with the deck gun. On 9 December, a happy crew was welcomed back to Fremantle after a very successful patrol.

Admiral Christie gave the Bowfin credit for sinking nine ships and five small schooners for a grand total of 71,000 tons. Postwar analysis reduced that number and gave her credit for sinking 26,000 tons and nine small craft. The real umber, most assuredly, lies somewhere in between. Even taking the most conservative estimate, it was a very good patrol. Griffith received the Navy Cross and the entire crew received a Presidential Unit Citation.

17 USS Seawolf 12th Patrol

By the end of 1943, the USS Seawolf was already legendary among submariners for her continuous 48-hour attack on a group of three cruisers near Christmas Island. "Fearless" Freddie Warder had been replaced in command by Commander Royce Gross; this patrol would show all that he was a worthy successor.

The boat was underway for the East China Sea from Midway on 26 December 1943. The patrol area was entered on 9 January 1944, and on the following day, they made their presence known.

Torpedo Attack #1

At 0936, smoke was sighted, and Captain Gross proceeded to close on its position. The source was identified as a seven freighter convoy with two escorts moving at eight knots at a range of 20,000 yards. Battle stations were called, and the Seawolf made a submerged approach.

At a range of 2000 yards the group made a zig, leaving one freighter in a good firing position. The Seawolf fired three torpedoes, resulting in two hits. A minute later, another explosion rang out. It's possible that the third shot hit a ship in the next column.

The entire convoy made a zig in Seawolf's direction except for the escorts, which remained on the far side. The largest ship in the bunch presented a good angle for the stern tubes, and all four were fired at the target from 3500 yards. Two hits were heard.

The captain swung the periscope to view the first target, which was now sinking. The second target showed no evidence of sinking but was stopped. A destroyer closed in on the Seawolf but Gross held the sub at periscope depth. The destroyer dropped several charges but none were close—it didn't have a good fix on the sub.

Commander Gross decided to remain submerged until after dark, and at that time, would attempt to finish off the second target. At 1827, the sub surfaced and picked up the target still stopped at 30,000 yards. The captain ordered her to move in to make visual contact. Another freighter had joined the ship and was starting to tow her, and a destroyer was also in the area. At 1500 yards, the captain fired three torpedoes—two at the towing ship; Gross then swung the boat around and fired all four stern torpedoes. Three hits were heard and the towing ship quickly disappeared. The other ship appeared much lower in the water also, so he assumed it had been hit by one of the shots.

A destroyer suddenly appeared at 1000 yards—she must have been behind the incapacitated ship to have appeared so quickly. The Seawolf went straight to 280 feet and made a hard left turn. Two hours later, the Seawolf surfaced and found all clear. After a quick battery charge, she headed back toward the damaged ship, which was still afloat. Passing through the wreckage of the towing ship, the captain made a surface approach; at 5200 yards, the sub was spotted and a destroyer headed toward it. Gross fired three forward torpedoes from this range and put on all four engines while turning away from the escort. Three hits were heard, and as they pulled to 12,000 yards away, the target disappeared from the radar screen.

Another escort appeared out of the darkness and was closing in on the sub. Gross took her down and underwent heavy depth charging. After spending more than 11 hours submerged, the Seawolf finally surfaced to find all clear.

Torpedo Attack # 2

Having only three torpedoes left—all forwards—Captain Gross went looking for an appropriate target. On 14 January, smoke was sighted around 0800, and an approach showed four freighters with two escorts. The sub tracked this group all day, and closed in after dark.

The first attack was foiled by a timely zig that left the Seawolf way out in left field. The sub surfaced and approached again. This time, the Seawolf had better luck.

Another setup was ruined by a zig, but immediately the ships turned again, this time presenting a good target if the Seawolf crew could set up fast enough.

The tracking party made the calculations in record time and the last three torpedoes were fired from 1500 yards. Two hits were scored and the ship was set ablaze. They came up for a gun action but could only fire six shots before being driven away by fire from several ships in the area. The light from the fire illuminated the sub, so Gross turned the boat and the fire illuminated the sub, so Gross turned the boat and headed away, securing from battle stations. The Seawolf continued to follow the group and called for help. The USS Whale, nearby, came on to attack the convoy and finish off the burning ship.

All torpedoes expended, the Seawolf headed back to Pearl.

18 USS Snook 5th Patrol

The USS Snook sank or damaged over 150,000 tons of Japanese shipping before being lost on her 9th patrol just before the war's end. Her hunting took her from the Kurile Ice Fields to the South China Sea and many areas in between.

Built in Portsmouth, New Hampshire, she was commissioned there on 24 October, 1942 and left shortly thereafter for her first war patrol. In January of 1944, she made a patrol into the South China Sea and had her best outing of the war. She departed Midway for her patrol area on 6 January 1944.

Torpedo Attack #1

Late in the evening of 23 January, a lone freighter with one escort steamed into view making nine knots. Since visibility was poor, Commander Charles Triebel decided to make a surface approach using sight and radar.

The target ship was heading almost due north and Snook approached on a course of 270 degrees, straight into her flank. When the sub reached a position about 1600 yards from the target, she opened fire with all six forward tubes. The crew listened quietly. The first three fish missed their mark, but torpedoes 4 and 5 hit the target and exploded. One minute later, the target exploded, and five minutes after that, it sank. The escort was completely incapacitated by the darkness and didn't pose a problem.

Torpedo Attack #2

The next attack occurred on the night of 8 February. Ten large freighters were contacted by radar at a range of about 22,000 yards. There were several escorts milling about also. Captain Triebel tracked the group on the surface for a while, and when the time for the attack came, he ordered the boat to submerge because it was a bright night.

The targets were more cooperative in moving into position, and once the range was less than 1000 yards, four stern torpedoes were fired. Two hits were scored on one freighter and one on another. Six minutes after the hit, a large explosion was heard from the first target, which then broke up several minutes later. Two escorts closed in and dropped 21 depth charges over a period of an hour, but none came close. By the time the Snook could return to the surface, the convoy had slipped away and the sub couldn't regain contact.

Torpedo Attack #3

Two days later on 10 February, another convoy was sighted. Captain Trieble allowed a properly marked hospital ship to pass and then noticed a destroyer heading straight toward them, its sonar pinging. The captain moved the Snook off the target track and fired four stern shots from long range on periscope data. Apparently, the Snook overestimated the size and speed of the destroyer—all torpedoes missed ahead of the target. The submarine went deep to avoid combat and lost contact with the convoy.

Torpedo Attack #4

A late night radar contact turned out to be a large unescorted freighter. The freighter wasn't zigging but continued straight on its base course. Captain Triebel approached boldly and fired three torpedoes from the surface at 1600 yards. Two hit but only one exploded. The one hit was enough to do the job. The target quickly disappeared from radar.

Torpedo Attack #5

On 15 February, a smoke contact developed into a small freighter also traveling alone. Without the fear of escorts, the Snook closed to 650 yards and fired two torpedoes. One hit and sent the freighter quickly to the bottom. The sub moved on to patrol just south of Korea.

Torpedo Attack #6

While en route back to Midway, the crew of the Snook contacted a friendly sub, which turned out to be the USS Plunger. The Snook surfaced to exchange information but immediately dived when smoke was sighted on the horizon.

The Snook approached the convoy from the south and the Plunger approached from the north. The Plunger was in position first and scored a hit that scattered the rest of the targets in the convoy. The two subs tracked the scattered freighters as well as they could during the next day and then surfaced at dark to attempt contact.

Although the Snook was below its safe fuel level for the return trip, the captain searched until contact was made with the convoy. Two freighters came into radar range escorted by at least 11 smaller ships. The sub weaved through the escorts and took up a firing position at a range of 3200 yards. A five-torpedo salvo was fired at two freighters. Two good hits were observed two minutes later. After a brief wait, a terrible explosion shook the boat and the targets disappeared from the radar screen.

Now the Snook made for Midway in earnest with very little fuel to spare.

19 USS Gunard 5th Patrol

The USS Gunard was one of the lesser known subs of the war; she had a respectable career during the war starting in the middle of 1943. Her best outing was her 5th patrol: During this sweep south of the Philippines, she sank one third of the ships she would sink for the entire war. The Gunard set out on this historic patrol on 16 April, 1944 under Charles Andrews.

Torpedo Attack #1

While patrolling on the surface on the morning of 6 May, the watch sighted a great deal of smoke on the horizon. Captain Andrews commenced his approach.

Tracking showed the sub to be about 19 miles off the track of the convoy. When Gunard drew a little closer, Captain Andrews saw merchant ships formed into three columns. There were at least six or seven escorts as well, but no planes were sighted. A glass smooth sea limited the number of periscope observations he could make safely, so the captain moved in mainly on information from the sound man.

After dodging the escorts, he picked a group of ships from the middle of the convoy to be his targets. At 1300, he fired three torpedoes at the first target and three more at the second target. All torpedoes were running normally, but they left trails of blue smoke that were spotted by a destroyer. The crew of the destroyer must have felt helpless as they watched all six torpedoes find targets. The two target ships each took two hits and two other overlapping ships each took a hit.

As the destroyer closed on the sub, the first two torpedoes hit. Noises of the ships breaking up were heard, and Captain Andrews assumed that the first two ships sank. He took the sub deep to wait out a shaking up from 98 depth charges before the Japanese broke off their attack. Back at periscope depth, the captain observed two ships in the process of sinking. A destroyer drove him deep again, and when he returned to the surface, only one ship was visible and it was on fire. The sub closed in. The captain ordered his men to finish her off with the deck gun, since all the destroyers had left.

After a fusillade of four-inch rounds, the ship refused to sink. Finally, the captain ordered up one more torpedo. Helped along by the torpedo hit and the ventilation provided by the deck gun, the last ship sank rather quickly.

Torpedo Attack #2

Patrolling was extremely calm until 17 May when a good sized target steamed into view. Rain squalls reduced visibility but made the scope almost impossible to see as the sub approached.

The target turned out to be a battleship with two destroyer escorts. All were zigging wildly and running at 23 knots. Commander Andrews had a hard time with the approach but finally managed to get with 2300 yards to fire all six forward torpedoes.

A faulty poppet valve almost caused the sub to breach after firing, and the negative ballast had to be flooded, which took the boat too deep for the periscope. The crew heard two hits as they headed deep; then the depth charges started to fall. Several were "too nicely placed for comfort," but the sub weathered the storm and came up to periscope depth to see the target departing, now at only 15 knots. She hadn't sunk, but maybe the Gunard had put her out of commission for a while.

Torpedo Attack #3

Rain, planes, and sub chasers were all the Gunard could find for several days until a sighting on 24 May just off the southern tip of Mindanao.

The captain approached the convoy of two small freighters and fired two torpedoes, which both missed. The freighters were running empty with a very shallow draft and the fish probably ran under them.

Escorts forced the sub down, but the depth charge attack was brief. When Commander Andrews brought his boat back to periscope depth, another group of ships was making an appearance. This turned out to be a much better group of targets: There were two good-size freighters and two tankers being guarded by three escorts. A quick approach was all that was needed, and the four loaded forward torpedoes were fired at a large tanker. Captain Andrews heard and saw three hits before he was forced deep by an escort.

The tanker was burning furiously. In all, 27 depth charges were dropped while the sound man listened to breaking-up noises from the direction of the target. When the sub was able to come up again, there were no signs of the target ship, and the others were steaming off at high speed.

An up-and-down routine of dodging planes followed for a number of days, and on 31 May, the routine was broken as three battleships came into view. The captain and crew made a valiant attempt to attack the group, but they were extremely disappointed. Unable to close to within firing range, the Gunard continued on to the south and arrived at Fremantle Australia on 11 June.

20 USS Sandlance 2nd Patrol

After coming off a successful 1st Patrol in the icy waters north of Japan with four confirmed sinkings, the captain and crew of the USS Sandlance were glad to head into the warmer waters of the Philippine Sea for the next patrol. Commander Garrison took the Sandlance out to sea on 20 April 1944 from Pearl Harbor, heading for the Mariana Islands.

Torpedo Attack #1

The crossing to the patrol area was quite uneventful, so crew members were well trained and rested by the time they made their first contact on 3 May, just north of Saipan.

They found a freighter with one escort. Commander Garrison watched as a setup went by the numbers. When the range closed to 1700 yards, he was ready to shoot. With a perfect 90-degree target track and torpedo gyro angles set at 0, he fired three shots. When the stopwatch held by the exec said there should be hits, there was nothing but silence. The Captain was shocked; He had been counting on three hits. The firing team reviewed the log and found an error in the target speed to account for the misses.

Now it was a race against the rising sun to get into position for another shot. At 0435, they moved in again on the target's flank and fired three torpedoes from 2300 yards. The escort made a halfhearted attack, but none of the depth charges fell close by.

The following day, the sub made an approach on what appeared to be a convoy, but it was only a group of small escort ships. Although the sub was in a favorable firing position, Commander Garrison held fire—the boats had such a shallow draft that torpedoes often ran right under them. He broke off the attack and withdrew.

Torpedo Attack #2

On 11 May, the captain was beginning to feel discouraged—he hadn't contacted a ship in nine days. Some other subs in the area were able to do some damage, but all the Sandlance got was the results of the "stirred-up hornet's nest." Heavy anti-submarine activity continued.

That afternoon, a ship's mast was spotted on the horizon. Commander Garrison turned in that direction to track. When the targets came "over the hill," he saw a large freighter and a large old gunboat, along with four escorts. He was going to fire at the gunboat but lost depth control and had to go deep. Two torpedoes were fired by sound bearings on the way down, but both missed.

The Sandlance crew heard two torpedoes hit the freighter, followed by loud breaking-up noises. The Sandlance then took a good pounding as the escorts and several planes all dropped depth charges on them at once. Except for a severe shaking up and some broken light bulbs, they incurred no damage.

Torpedo Attack #3

On 14 May, the submarine had moved just south of Guam and contacted a small convoy. The captain moved in for a short-range submerged shot from 1400 yards. Four torpedoes were fired at the leading freighter for two timed hits. An escort bore down, preventing Commander Garrison from swinging around to use the stern tubes, and the sub headed deep.

Avoiding the escorts put the sub closer to the damaged ship. The popping and breaking-up noises were so loud, the captain was afraid the target was sinking right on top of them. There was no doubt that the ship sank. The sub went down to 450 feet and maneuvered away from the escorts.

Since their attempt to use the stern tubes had been foiled, they were left with eight torpedoes in the rear, and none in the forward tubes. Future attacks would be awkward.

Torpedo Attack #4

Back in the Saipan area on 16 May, the sub made contact at dusk with several ships. The next several hours were a constant duel with a radar plane, which forced the sub down several times, preventing an end-around maneuver. But the plane was only able to follow the ships for 50 miles.

Once the convoy was out to sea, the Sandlance came up and made the maneuver, moving into firing position at midnight. The captain swung the rear end around and fired four shots at a large freighter from 2800 yards and then went deep. Two good hits were observed and the following depth charge attack was very light. The entire crew heard the breaking-up noises.

After avoiding the escorts, they surfaced to chase the convoy but couldn't regain contact.

Torpedo Attack #5

Smoke was seen on the horizon the following morning. The sub raced ahead at full speed on an end-around. Later, a plane came out of the clouds and had a perfect shot at the Sandlance as she scrambled to dive. The pilot wasn't up to the task, however, and missed the sub by several hundred yards.

Sandlance returned to the surface and continued trying to get ahead of the ships. This went on until after dark when the sub made radar contact with the group at 20,000 yards. It was too dark to use the periscope, so they slowly approached on the surface, finding two large ships stopped and two escorts patrolling around them. At 3000 yards, the captain turned the boat for a stern shot. As he was about to fire, one of the target ships turned a search light on the Sandlance and Commander Garrison was forced to dive, firing four torpedoes on the way down. One sure hit was heard, but other torpedo hits may have been lost in the noise of the depth charge explosions that followed.

An hour later when the Sandlance surfaced, the damaged ship was half underwater and burning fiercely. Having disposed of the stern torpedoes in a fine manner, the Sandlance headed for Fremantle and a refit.

21 USS Barb 8th Patrol

The USS Barb was launched from Groton, Connecticut, in April 1942. Unlike many of the subs launched during the war, she didn't get off to a flying start; in fact, she wasn't credited with her first official sinking until May 1944. Once the Barb finally got going, however, she quickly made up for lost time with a series of successful patrols.

The first of this string was her 8th patrol, which started on 21 May 1944, when she sailed from Midway to patrol off the northern tip of the Empire in the Sea of Okhotsk with Commander Buckley in command.

Torpedo Attack #1

On 31 May, the watch spotted a large tanker, and Commander Buckley commenced the approach. He had to withdraw when it was noticed that the tanker was showing proper Russian lights. Later, when the haze finally lifted, a large merchant ship came into view.

An air attack forced the Barb down, but she quickly popped back up to periscope depth to fire three torpedoes at the target. With a range of only 1400 yards and a small gyro angle, the shots looked good. Several hits were scored amidships, and steam rushed out of the opened hull as the 1000-ton merchant ship sank.

Immediately after the sinking, a passenger-cargo ship came into view and picked up a number of survivors of the attack. Commander Buckley decided against a gun attack due to aircraft in the area and a large-caliber machine gun on the target ship. Instead, he made a quick end-around to attack from the port quarter. At 1000 yards off the target track, he pulled the plug and went to periscope depth.

The target came nicely into view, so Captain Buckley quickly swung the rear around to use some stern torpedoes while he had the chance. At 1600 yards, he opened fire with three shots. All three torpedoes hit, opening the ship up from one end to the other. The 3800-ton ship followed the first target to the bottom.

Torpedo Attack #2

The captain and crew learned a valuable lesson about attacking lone high-speed targets on 2 June, when the Barb approached a rapidly moving solitary ship. As the target sped past, she fired three torpedoes set to run shallow. All three missed, probably passing under the target.

Of course, the target turned out to be a destroyer, which turned and followed the trail of the torpedoes back to the Barb with its guns blazing and depth-charge throwers and racks in action. The destroyer gave the Barb quite a scare before turning and leaving the attack to continue its urgent business elsewhere.

The crew of the Barb patrolled on the surface among the ice flows for the rest of the day, feeling safe from observers because of the glare of the sun off the ice.

Torpedo Attack #3

The Barb moved further into the Sea of Okhotsk and patrolled the shipping lanes near the La Perous Strait, where constant mist and fog reduced visibility to almost zero. On 11 June, she sank two trawlers with the gun after a chase through the ice fields.

After the gun action, the watch saw two smoke streaks on the horizon. A four-hour chase brought them even with a two-ship convoy consisting of one large and one medium-sized freighter. It was one of the blackest nights the captain had ever seen. Visibility was very limited, but Commander Buckley was able to use the radar to keep tabs on the targets while he moved into position. He fired three torpedoes at the first ship from 1600 yards, and then swung and fired three more at the second ship, which was now at 1900 yards. The first ship took one hit and slowed considerably; the second took two solid hits and sank stern first.

Commander Buckley then turned back to the damaged ship, which had unleashed a gun amidships. The captain ordered the lookouts and quartermaster below and continued on the surface. He maneuvered for a good broadside shot at the crippled ship. Finally, it presented its side to them and the captain turned hard to use the stern tubes. He fired the 7, 8, and 9 tubes for three perfect hits. The target, which was only traveling at half a knot, suddenly blew sky-high—a torpedo must have touched one of the target's magazines. Once again, the Barb was alone on the surface.

Torpedo Attack #4

On 13 June, the captain was again faced with "whitish" visibility conditions, due to the ice. He again took advantage of the situation to patrol on the surface, increasing his camouflage by tying a white sheet to the periscope shears to hide the dark gray paint.

Around 1700 hours, the watch sighted smoke. Captain Buckley set a course to move ahead of the target. He followed until after dark and adjusted the course to match the target's new zig-zag plan. The night was very dark, but because the water was extremely luminescent, the captain decided he would have to attack from a stopped position, using the stern tubes. The stern tubes were chosen so the Barb would be pointing in the right direction for a getaway.

The Barb stopped dead ahead of the target and waited for the expected zig. The wake from the bow looked huge as the ship closed in on them; finally, it made a zig, leaving them in perfect firing position.

The last two stern torpedoes were fired from 1475 yards. One hit amidships and the other blew off part of the ship's fantail. The ship stopped and started to settle by the aft with its whistle blowing. An escort then appeared, And it was a race to get away. Just as it appeared that the escort would overtake the sub, it turned away and returned to the sinking ship.

After waiting several hours, Commander Buckley saw that the target wasn't going to sink, so he headed back in to finish her off. The target sank by itself as they were making the approach.

The rest of the patrol was spent surveying the area and taking pictures. On 4 July, they arrived at Midway.

22 USS Barb 9th Patrol

The 9th patrol of the USS Barb could very well have been much higher on the list of best patrols ranked by tonnage sunk, but many of her targets were taken off the official list after the war. Even so, the official total for this patrol put her and the captain., Commander E.B. Fluckey, fifth on the list.

The patrol started on 10 August 1944 with the sub's departure from Midway, heading for the Luzon Straits near the Philippines. It was part of a three-boat wolf pack that included the USS Tunny and the USS Queenfish.

Torpedo Attack #1

The patrol was very routine and uneventful until early in the morning on 31 August. A convoy came into sight just north of Luzon, and as the Barb was approaching with the other boats in her wolf pack, the radar operator picked up interference from three other radars of similar type. This indicated that another U.S. wolf pack was also tracking the group. Captain Fluckey said it "looked like a three-ring circus was about to start with two wolf packs and one convoy." Several torpedo hits were heard as the Barb maneuvered to gain a good firing position.

By the time the convoy closed to within visible range of the Barb, several ships had already sunk, but there were still at least eight afloat, including escorts. The largest ship left was a freighter in the middle of the group, which Fluckey chose along with a nearby tanker as targets.

At 0624, he was in a good firing position with a chance to wipe out an entire column of ships. Then, it all came apart as the other subs started shooting. Two torpedoes were heard running close by and the nearest escort took the hits and blew up. Two more torpedoes were heard running and one was headed directly toward the Barb.

The captain ducked the periscope, letting the fish swim over the boat. The large freighter turned to evade at this point, but Captain Fluckey swung his stern tubes to bear and fired all four torpedoes. The first two hit the freighter with considerable effect; the third missed the freighter but hit a small tanker in the next column.

The Barb turned hard to line up a target with the bow tubes, but by the time she was set up, the ships were all out of range. Captain Fluckey turned back to the damaged freighter, but it was already sinking, stern first. Several planes arrived and began dropping bombs, and the escorts were all sliding depth charges off the racks. None were close to the Barb.

The Barb continued to chase the group, but at 1250, the watch could no longer see the smoke, and Captain Fluckey gave up the high-speed chase.

Torpedo Attack #2

About an hour later, at 1349, the sub was back in business. Smoke was sighted and another high-speed chase began. This was probably one of the ships scattered by the merry-go-round attack that morning. Although the engineer was concerned about the batteries, the captain continued to approach at high speed submerged.

At 1730, while looking for escorts with the periscope, the Barb encountered the "latest fiendish antisubmarine weapon" of the Japanese—a large bird! Each time the scope was raised, the bird perched upon it and draped its tail feathers over the window. Needless to say, this proved extremely confusing to the approach officer. He banged the scope, shook it, and ducked it under but the bird hung on and hovered over until the scope came back up. Finally, the officer raised both scopes, thereby disorienting the bird long enough to get a good reading. The bird, of course, was photographed for the anitsubmarine file.

At 1752, all tubes were made ready. The Barb waited for the suspected zig. At 1300 yards the ship made the turn and three bow torpedoes were fired. All three hit. Fifteen or so lookouts on the catwalk in front of the bridge of the Japanese freighter were knocked into the drink, and when the second and third torpedoes hit, the ship broke in two and rapidly sank.

When too many members of the crew were allowed to view the sinking ship, a subchaser spotted the scope and turned to attack. Captain Fluckey took the sub deep and sat out a bone-jarring depth charge attack.

The Barb and the Tunny cleared the area to head toward quieter waters.

Torpedo Attack #3

The next several days were spent avoiding very persistent radar-equipped aircraft. A number of depth bombs were dropped on the Barb—several uncomfortably close.

The sub moved on to patrol in the Bashi Channel, south of Taiwan. On 8 September, the Barb received a call from the Queenfish about a convoy in the area. Captain Fluckey poured on the fuel to catch it. After tracking the convoy into the morning of 9 September, he was unable to close and the group passed them by. Disappointed by the close call, the captain turned his attention to a trailer that appeared, thinking he might be able to close on that target.

The ship turned out to be a Chidori-class destroyer, but the captain was determined to shoot at something. He expressed his reservations about attacking the target, but then added, "However, once in every submariner's life there comes the urge to let three fish go, particularly after a convoy skids across his nose while his hands are tied, I dood it."

At 3000 yards, he fired tubes 1, 2 and 3. All three missed. He evaded the destroyer at high speed on the surface, but planes too numerous to count entered the fight and he was forced to dive. By the time he surfaced again, the convoy was hopelessly out of reach and so he returned to patrol.

Once again, the Barb was constantly harassed by planes. The sub's log had reached Plane Contact number 67 on 14 September when radar picked up targets at 0003 in the morning. Barb commenced the approach.

Torpedo Attack #4

The targets turned out to be two Chidori-class destroyers. The captain hadn't learned his lesson from the first encounter, so he headed in on the surface to attack.

At a range of only 1380 yards, he fired three torpedoes. It looked like a snap, but all three missed and the destroyers turned to attack the sub. The Barb headed away at high speed on the surface with the destroyers following.

A torpedo attack on one of the destroyer's starboard flank made the ship turn away. Apparently the Queenfish had come to the rescue.

The torpedoes missed but caused the escort to shift its attention. Captain Fluckey attempted a difficult narrow angle shot with two torpedoes—both missed. He then took the boat deep. The misses were chalked up to expert sound men on the target ships.

On 16 September, Captain Fluckey received orders to go at high speed to an area where a U.S. sub had sunk a Japanese transport ship that was carrying Australian and

British POWs. They left immediately and prepared the boat to take on 100 survivors, if necessary.

Torpedo Attack #5

While en route to pick up the survivors, the Barb came across another convoy being tracked by the Queenfish. Having a good position, Captain Fluckey decided to delay briefly to see if he could attack. He came in on the starboard bow of what seemed to be a group of tankers. Fluckey moved in on the largest pip on the radar and at 2325 exclaimed, "ye Gods! It's a flat top!" He came in with a good angle and maneuvered so that there were several ships overlapping, which formed about 1000 feet of targets.

All tubes were made ready, and at 2332, all six bow tubes were emptied. An escort spotted the sub, so Captain Fluckey took it deep. The crew heard to hits on a tanker and three on the carrier. When they heard breaking-up noises, it was obvious that one ship had sunk—possibly both. No one could be certain which ship went down. Captain Fluckey thought it was the carrier, but the captain of the Queenfish said it was the tanker. They would sort it out after the war.

Having been side tracked for five hours, they surfaced at the first chance and once again headed for the survivors. The captain later said that he would have gladly given up the pleasure of sinking the carrier to rescue just one of the men they eventually picked up.

On 17 September, the Barb picked up 14 survivors who had spent five long days and nights in the sea. They were covered with oil, which probably saved their lives. Too much credit cannot be given to the captain and crew of the Barb for their efforts in rescuing and tending to the 14 men they saved. They carried the men through the boat from one location to another until all were cleaned up, tended to by the pharmacist's mate, fed, and put to bed in bunks. Many were too weak to thank the crew of the Barb, but their tear-filled eyes spoke to all who were aboard in a way that would never be forgotten.

With this very valuable cargo abroad, the Barb headed to Saipan.

The investigation after the war turned the official record of this patrol upside down. The captain claimed to sink four ships for a tonnage total of 42,050 tons. This was later increased to 47,050 tons as a second ship in the first attack was confirmed sunk.

After the war, however, most of the sinkings weren't allowed, but the carrier was added to the list. The final total was three ships sunk for a total of 36,800 tons. It's almost certain that several other ships were sunk during this patrol as they were witnessed going down by the captain, the commander of the wolf pack who was aboard, and many of the bridge crew.

23 USS Barb 11th Patrol

After a quick refit at Midway following her 10th patrol, the Barb was out again on 19 December 1944 for another legendary patrol. She headed out in company of the Queenfish and the Picuda. Their patrol area would be the Formosa Strait and the China Sea.

Transit to the patrol area would be quiet, so the crew celebrated Christmas by singing carols and exploding a floating mine with gunfire.

On the morning of 7 January, the watch sighted a large convoy on radar. Visibility was poor and a thick haze hung on the water. Captain Fluckey slowly moved onto the target track and waited. The sound man heard loud screws but there wasn't a ship in sight as the captain wildly swung the periscope around.

Then, at 0902, the haze lifted showing the Barb to be right in the middle of the convoy. A large tanker and a freighter were in good line for a shot so the tubes were made ready, but the two ships made a zig away from the sub, which made the shot doubtful.

A destroyer crossed 1000 yards ahead—an easy and provocative shot, but the captain had finally learned his lesson about such tactics, having wasted 12 torpedoes in the last three patrols on fast-moving, shallow-draft, and maneuverable destroyers. He was forced to grit his teeth and let the convoy pass in hopes of surfacing later and making an end-around. He sent a contact report and one of the other subs got into position and scored hits. The Barb continued to patrol in the shipping lanes.

Torpedo Attack #1

Just after noon on 16 January, the watch spotted smoke. The other subs were contacted as the Barb began her end-around maneuver. By 1600, the sub had good contact on at least eight ships. Captain Fluckey was waiting for the Picuda to make contact before attacking. When word came from the Picuda that she was in position, the Barb submerged and commenced the attack.

The convoy was in several columns, surrounded by escorts. The most important ship appeared to a large four goal-poster transport. It seemed a snap to get into the middle of the group, but the captain chose to attack from the shore side of the ships to prevent them from escaping into shallow water and to force them to run toward the other subs.

Now in position, the captain took one more look and fired three torpedoes at the large four-goal-poster and three more at another freighter in the column. The crew heard four torpedo hits in close succession, followed by a huge explosion that rocked the boat as it was turning to use its stern tubes. The second target disappeared with the explosion. The transport was half afloat with her stern sticking up in the air, her bow obviously resting in the mud. Captain Fluckey took the sub deep to avoid an escort that suddenly appeared.

When the danger appeared to be over, he returned to the surface and took off after the rest of the convoy. The Picuda with the last ships in the group and headed in on "our normal screaming surface approach." At 2180 yards, the Barb fired three torpedoes: two at one ship and another at an overlapping freighter. All three hit their targets. The first ship sank and remaining two ships in the area maintained formation but increased speed. There were nine escorts around the group.

A quick move back toward the ships brought the convoy into view and captain Fluckey fired three torpedoes from a distance of 1590 yards. The sub was swinging to the right in order to ease out and use the stern tubes when all three torpedoes hit, resulting in a tremendous explosion. The pressure wave was literally breathtaking: A high vacuum resulted. In the boat, the shirts of the crew in the conning tower were pulled over their heads by the air rushing out of the hatch. A quick look showed both targets to be gone, along with many of the escorts. The captain decided not to claim these as sunk: Four ships sunk with 12 torpedoes was about all "traffic will bear."

The Picuda and Queenfish finished off the attack and they all withdrew to continue patrol. Aircraft kept them hopping, and several convoys were sighted, but non were close enough to attack. They continued to sweep the approaches to the Formosa Strait.

Shipping in the area had virtually dried up. The Allied sub and air attack had made the Japanese very cautious. The Axis convoys were traveling close to shore in shallow water during the day and pulling into harbors at night.

The Barb received a convoy contact report and began to search down the estimated track. When the group couldn't be found, Captain Fluckey assumed the convoy was anchored for the night, and so began a dangerous shallow water search. He hit the jackpot.

On the night of 27 January, he rounded a group of islands and picked up at least 30 ships deep in a harbor. Before beginning the attack, Captain Fluckey took the following information into account:

- There were few junks in the area—junks normally avoided mined areas.
- There was evidence of Japanese radar operating in the area.
- Visibility was poor.
- Since anchored ships always point into the wind, they would present a 60-degree angle—a fair angle for an attack.
- He could retire through a mass of junks he had spotted earlier, making it hard for the escorts to follow him.
- He would have to run on the surface for an hour before reaching water deep enough to dive. The attack would have to be a complete surprise.

The captain liked the odds. He called the crew to battle stations.

Torpedo Attack #2

As he moved in, the captain's biggest problem was how to keep from sending too many torpedoes into the same ship. With so many targets, he couldn't fail to hit something.

At 0404, he fired the last four bow torpedoes and swung hard around. There were only five fathoms of water beneath the keel. With the bow now around, tubes 7, 8, 9, and 10 were emptied. All ahead flank!

All eight torpedoes were seen and heard to explode. A large freighter was seen to take two hits and sink. A ship in the second column took one hit and was damaged. Another freighter in the third column caught torpedo 4—it burst into flames and sank. Several other ships were hit, two of which blew up immediately and the crew breathed easily for the first time in hours.

Rain and bad weather hindered them for the next several days, and then they returned to Midway.

This was a truly legendary performance. Commander Fluckey received the Congressional Medal of Honor for his daring attack on the ships in the harbor, and although his record was decimated after the war, he claimed to have sunk nine ships for a total of 60,000 tons. He actually saw most of these ships sink, but his official total was cut to show only 4 1/3 ships sunk, for a total of

24,000 tons. This is another case in which we'll give the captain the benefit of the doubt.

24 USS Harder 5th Patrol

" The most brilliant submarine patrol of the war...." The normally conservative language of official navy reports was dropped when describing this patrol. Harder's 5th war patrol was the high point of her successful career.

The Harder only had one commanding officer—Lt. Commander S.D. Dealey. He took command of the sleek craft when it was placed into commission on 2 December 1942 and went down with her while on patrol less than two years later. In recognition of his superior work as commanding officer, Dealey was awarded the Medal of Honor, the Silver Star, the Navy Cross, and three Gold

Stars in lieu of his second, third, and fourth Navy Crosses. He and his crew also won the Presidential Unit Citation.

During his 4th patrol, Dealey had good luck attacking destroyers, and he used his new knowledge and confidence from this to specialize in destroyers during the 5th patrol. The Harder sailed from Fremantle to cruise in the area around the Sibutu Passage north of the Celebes Sea on 26 May 1944.

Torpedo Attack #1

On 6 June, Commander Dealey made his first effort to transit the Sibutu passage, a heavily patrolled bottleneck of shipping traffic. Trying to run the passage on the surface at night, he came across a rich convoy also attempting the crossing at night.

He began his chase. The fast moving group was composed of three large tankers and two destroyers. When Captain Dealey's sub was still 16,000 yards away from the convoy, the moon suddenly broke through the low clouds and the Harder was left sitting in plain view.

The nearest destroyer turned hard and put on 24 knots in an attempt to catch the sub, which was already fleeing the area. The sub's wake made it easy for the pursuing escort to follow and close the gap. When it became apparent they couldn't outrun the destroyer and that it wasn't going to quit the chase after scaring them off, Dealey decided to go on the offensive. He took the boat down and pulled quickly off the track.

After a few minutes, the destroyer came steaming down the old track, straight into Harder's ambush. Dealey fired three torpedoes. The first missed but the next two scored solid hits and sent the destroyer to the bottom, stern first, leaving only a cloud of smoke on the water.

A second destroyer closed in on the sub. Captain Dealey gave it six bow torpedoes. This time the escort was ready. She managed to avoid the shots and went on to give the Harder a good going-over with depth charges.

Later that night, the sub surfaced to try another approach, only this time they were foiled by Mother Nature—the "ship" they were approaching turned out to be a small island, which they realized after knocking out a chunk of the island's shallow reef.

Torpedo Attack #2

Later that night, well down the passage, the Harder was spotted by a night-flying patrol plane. The plane called for a destroyer, which arrived shortly, but Harder was waiting for it.

As the destroyer entered the area, the Harder silently closed on it and fired three torpedoes from a scant 650 yards. Two of the fish hit the destroyer amidships. The Harder moved out of the area as a huge explosion ripped the destroyer apart. Another escort soon arrived and pinned the Harder to the bottom for over two hours with one depth charge attack after another.

Destroyers now flooded the area—no less than ten were seen during the next day, and sometimes as many as six were in view at one time. Dealey headed toward Borneo for a special mission.

The next night, he pulled close to shore and sent a team in to pick up several British intelligence officers, using collapsible canoes. The mission went off without a hitch, but now the submarine had to go back through the Sibutu Passage. Two destroyers were patrolling the entrance, which was only six miles from the fleet anchorage at Tawi Tawi.

Torpedo Attack #3

Rather than waiting to sneak past after the destroyers moved out of position, Dealey watched until he knew their patrol pattern and then went in to attack. He waited until the ships presented an overlapping target and then fired four shots from 1000 yards at the leading escort. The first shot missed in front, the next two scored solid hits, and the last torpedo missed astern. The captain ordered hard rudder to swing the boat around to use the stern tubes, but before he was able to set up, he was surprised to see the last torpedo hit the second destroyer.

The first ship exploded when the cool water hit the boilers; it headed toward the bottom. The second ship nosed over; with its stern sticking straight up in the air, it sank as well.

Fifteen minutes later, air cover arrived and bombed the area looking for the Harder, but she had already moved on. She was heading toward Tawi Tawi to see if some large ships from the fleet were in the area.

Torpedo Attack #4

At 1700, the watch sighted a large task force and Captain Dealey called his crew to battle stations. Three battleships, four cruisers, and at least six destroyers came into view. As Harder was sneaking in to attack, a patrol plane spotted her and directed a destroyer to her position.

Dealey decided that a depth charge attack was inevitable, so he lined the oncoming destroyer up for a down-the-throat shot. Soon he passed the point of no return, if he didn't hit the rushing ship, Harder would certainly be sunk.

With the range down to 1500 yards, he fired three bow tubes and ordered the sub to go deep. All three hit with a tremendous explosion. As they passed 80 feet, the destroyer blew up directly over them. Gear went flying, the mooring chain was pulled loose, and all aboard were knocked from their feet. The explosion was much stronger than any depth charge attack.

As the other escorts entered the fray and started dropping depth charges, one of the British officers was heard to say, "I say, old boy, would you mind taking us back to Borneo?"

His mission complete, Captain Dealey headed back to Australia.

25 USS Spadefish 1st Patrol

The Spadefish came along rather late in the war. Her keel was laid at the Navy Yard in Mare Island, California on 27 May 1943. Roughly a year later, on 8 May 1944, her first sea trials were conducted in the vicinity of San Francisco Bay.

Sound contact with the escort ship was lost during the dive, but the crew continued the testing. They surfaced several hours later to find that the escort had departed and that the Spadefish was rumored to be lost in 1200 feet of water. This wouldn't be the last time the tough Spadefish would repudiate such rumors.

To Sea

By 14 June 1944, crew training and boat modifications were complete and she sailed for Pearl Harbor. There, she joined with several other boats to head out into enemy waters under the Commander Gordon W. Underwood.

On 13 August, she sailed into an intense storm. The seas were so rough that periscope sightings couldn't be made without broaching the surface with the boat. Even at 150 feet, the boat would occasionally roll as much as 25 degrees. The bad weather continued and by 17 August, the Spadefish was about 70 miles south of Formosa in the Bashi Channel.

Frequent aircraft sightings keep the lookouts sharp. Late that evening, Underwood received a message from the USS Picuda about a sighting by the USS Redfish of a 13-ship convoy in the area. Captain Underwood hurried to start the search based on the contact report. It quickly became obvious that bad weather had fouled up everyone's navigation: He found the USS Picuda where he thought the USS Redfish was, and the convoy was nowhere to be seen.

Early in the morning on 18 August, the Spadefish received the word from the Redfish that she was about to attack the convoy from the starboard flank. Captain Underwood thought he had finally found the convoy on radar, but it turned out to be several small islands just south of the Balintang Channel. The search was continued to the southwest.

More enemy planes were spotted, but finally, all this wandering around paid off. At 1048, the sound man picked up pinging and screw sounds in the direction of the channel.

Apparently, a convoy was coming down the channel headed for Luzon. The convoy turned south and away from the Spadefish, so she surfaced and headed down the possible convoy route.

Torpedo Attack #1

Later that night, at 2158, a contact was picked up on radar and the crew went to battle stations. The contact developed into a single, unescorted ship. Visibility was zero, but contact was maintained via radar. After several hours of pursuing the zigging target, Captain Underwood fired four torpedoes from a submerged position at a range of 3040 yards. All missed. Underwood suspected the trails had been seen due to the highly phosphorescent nature of the water. Several explosions, thought to be depth charges, sent the Spadefish deep. When she surfaced, the contact had been lost. Shortly thereafter, another single ship appeared. The USS Rasher had attacked the convoy and the scattered ships had run straight to the waiting Spadefish.

They commenced an end-around maneuver and took up a position 7500 yards ahead of the target. It looked like a large transport. A large zig toward the Spadefish put her in good firing position, and with a target range of 2500 yards, Underwood fired all six forward torpedoes—he didn't want to miss again! Gyro angle was 335 degrees.

The first and second shots hit. A loud explosion followed, and the target disappeared from the radar. Breaking-up noises were heard for several minutes.

The following morning, the watch spotted another ship. Captain Underwood chased it, but aircraft prevented the Spadefish from surfacing. Eventually, the quarry was lost, and at that point, Underwood decided he was a long way from where he was supposed to be and headed back toward Formosa.

Torpedo Attack #2

On 27 August, the watch saw several masts on the horizon and the captain called the crew to battle stations. A small convoy was heading out to sea through the Babuyan Channel and the Spadefish was in a perfect position.

Captain Underwood set a standard approach course and closed in. The targets proved to be three large tankers riding empty. Two escorts were picked up on sound but must have been far ahead—they couldn't be seen. Underwood and crew performed a perfect approach and took a position ahead of the targets, just off their track. They waited. A small zig put the Spadefish between the second and third ships. Three forward torpedoes were fired at a range of 1960 yards at the second ship, and two hits were scored.

The sound man reported that the screws had stopped. Underwood quickly turned is attention to the third ship and fired three stern torpedoes. One scored a hit. He fired a fourth torpedo to score another. By now, escorts and aircraft were heading into the area, so Underwood ordered the sub to surface, he found one of the tankers sunk and one beached in a small bay being guarded by a destroyer.

Underwood spent the better part of a day trying to sneak into the bay to finish off the tanker. At one point, he did get into a firing position on the destroyer and fired his last four aft torpedoes. All missed. Low on torpedoes then, the Spadefish headed for Saipan for a reload.

Torpedo Attack #3

The Spadefish was back on station by 6 September, just to the east of Formosa. On the morning of 8 September, she was back in business as the watch sighted smoke on the horizon and the sound man picked up pinging in that direction.

The target turned out to be an eight-ship convoy with at least three escorts, and was making good speed at eight knots. Captain Underwood couldn't close submerged, so he set a course to trail for a while.

As darkness fell, he surfaced to overtake the convoy. Previously, he had been worried about enemy radar and had attacked submerged even at night; this time, however, he decided to ignore the radar and fight from the surface.

The Spadefish performed an end-around on the zigging convoy. The base course was determined to be 105 degrees. Underwood closed in on the two-column convoy from the flank and fired from about 2000 yards away. He fired first at the last ship in the far column and then at the last ship in the near column, the largest in the convoy.

Both targets were hit, the first disintegrating upon impact and the second settling quickly. Underwood turned the boat to bring the stern tubes to bear and fired four shots at a target in the middle of the column. He heard two hits. Depth charges started to fall, but the Spadefish crossed behind to the other side of the convoy without being spotted.

Underwood headed in for another attack, now aided by the rising moon. He fired three shots at each of two targets framed nicely by the moon. He hit the first ship, and it blew up, but he missed the second after receiving faulty range information from the radar. Once again, the boat was turned to bring the stern tubes into use. Four torpedoes were fired at a transport; two hit. This ship didn't sink, however. It was last seen beating a slow retreat, low in the water and smoking.

Another escort arrived, and shell and depth-charge attacks became more intense, but the Spadefish was well away from danger. Unfortunately, as she withdrew, the wake was spotted and a destroyer was on her tail. Underwood tried to shake it but finally had to go deep. He later surfaced and tried to attack again but the convoy had moved in too close to shore. He ordered the crew to secure from battle stations.

The sub continued to patrol around the mouth of a small harbor, when a small inter-island freighter came into view and the captain fired four torpedoes. The freighter must have had a very shallow draft. All shots missed, probably passing under the ship. Again, depth charges started falling, so Underwood wisely left the area.

The Spadefish continued to ride herd on the convoy for several days, but it refused to leave the safety of the harbor. Finally, she left the area to meet with the USS Redfish and USS Picuda to exchange information. Leaving the convoy in their very good hands, the Spadefish headed back to Pearl Harbor for a much deserved rest, arriving on September 24. She had been at sea for 63 days. In all the Spadefish fired 45 torpedoes, resulting in 15 hits.

26 USS Spadefish 2nd Patrol

After a much deserved rest and an intense training period, the Spadefish headed out to sea for her second war patrol on 23 October 1944. She was again accompanied by two other boats, the USS Sunfish and the USS Peto. With the Spadefish in command, they were known as "Underwood's Urchins."

Their assigned area for this patrol was the heavily traveled Yellow Sea. After a stop at Midway for fuel, the subs headed out. The Spadefish, however, quickly developed a knock in one prop shaft. A mooring line had been dropped overboard upon her departure from Midway and it must have somehow become tangled in the linkage. After turning and heading back to Midway, a diver quickly cleared the prop and they were back on their way at top speed.

The three boats quietly made their way into the Yellow Sea undetected. On 12 November, Underwood received a report of two U.S. Planes down in his area and spent the next several days off the coast of Shanghai looking for the pilots. Fortunately, this search was a success.

Torpedo Attack #1

The next day, the watch sighted smoke for the first time on the patrol, and shortly thereafter, a converted ore carrier came into view with an escort. The attack was well planned, but just as they were about to shoot, the carrier turned wildly and the escort headed straight for them. Caught in very shallow water, the Spadefish evaded at two-thirds speed while the escort dropped 19 depth charges in less than two minutes. The escort captain apparently thought he had destroyed the Spadefish and remained in the area for some time looking for wreckage and survivors. Undoubtedly, the Spadefish was once again reported as sunk. Two more escorts arrived and Underwood wisely decided to leave the area.

He didn't leave permanently, however—the next evening he surfaced to find a large freighter with oil drums on deck under tow by a smaller ship with three escorts. The convoy was zigzagging only mildly, but the towed ship was having a hard time with it.

Underwood crossed to the open side of the group and fired five bow torpedoes from a range of 3000 yards. Four of the five hit and the freighter burst into flames. The holocaust lit the entire area. Underwood quickly retreated to watch from a distance the fire, with the escorts milling about, occasionally dropping charges.

The sub surfaced on 14 November and headed over the shallow Yangtze Banks. The circular currents in the Yellow Sea made this area a gathering place for flotsam. Only by maintaining a constant lookout was the sub able to avoid several loose-floating mines.

Torpedo Attack #2

Things were slow for several days. On 16 November, the lookouts reported a waterspout as smoke on the horizon. The following afternoon, they were rewarded with the real thing. At 1434, smoke was spotted and at last four ships were visible by 1642. One of these turned out to be an aircraft carrier. The ships were heading straight for the Spadefish.

Realizing it would soon be dark, Underwood decided to let the group pass right over and then attack it on the surface at night. He went to 150 feet, and at 1720 the convoy passed over. The sound of the screws was punctuated by the pinging of the escorts' sonar. Half an hour later, back at periscope depth, he could see five large cargo ships trailed by the carrier. One of the ships was a large tanker and the rest were large freighters. A number of other warships—destroyers and smaller escorts—were present.

At 1843, Underwood surfaced and sent his men to battle stations. By 2119, he had slipped by several escorts and pulled even with the carrier. He set up to attack from the starboard flank, but the carrier took a zig away and he had to head out again to set up for another try. Thirty-nine minutes later, he again slipped behind the escort and set up for a shot on the tanker. After a five-minute setup, he fired six torpedoes at the carrier at a range of 4100 yards. Underwood then turned to port to bring the large tanker into line with the stern tubes and fired all four stern torpedoes.

Four of the six torpedoes hit the carrier. She spewed forth a mass of flames and began to settle by the stern. Planes rolled off the flight deck and into the sea as the ship listed to starboard. A last look at the carrier Jinyo showed her blazing bow pointing skyward and her stern settling on the bottom in 23 fathoms of water. One torpedo struck home on the tanker, but she wasn't seriously damaged and was able to maintain her position in the convoy.

Torpedo Attack #3

There were still several large ships left, so the Spadefish wasn't finished yet. Shortly after midnight, she drove back in for another attack. This time she was spotted by the escorts, and tracer bullets flew around the Spadefish bridge as Captain Underwood calmly ordered the boat to turn. He unloaded the stern tubes at a large destroyer, the nearest target, and was rewarded by several explosions. The ship disappeared in a cloud of smoke. He ordered the sub, still on the surface, to emergency flank speed and gradually pulled away from the chasing escorts.

Things were slow for a number of days as the Spadefish showed up late for several encounters only to find escorts picking up survivors of another sub's attacks. After a couple of days on lifeguard duty, watching for downed U.S. pilots after a large bombing mission, she made her last score of the patrol.

Torpedo Attack #4

On 29 November, the watch spotted a single ship on radar. It was zig-zagging on a base course of 160 degrees at about seven knots. Captain Underwood approached submerged to a range of 3500 yards. The target was a heavily loaded freighter. Four shots were fired and two struck home; the freighter sank almost immediately. Having only one torpedo left, Spadefish headed for home. The trip back was uneventful save for the birth of six pups by the ship's dog, Luau.

27 USS Spadefish 5th Patrol

After a successful 3rd patrol, it was decided that Underwood had commanded more than his share of combat patrols. He was relieved of command and replaced by Commander W. S. Germerhausen, who commanded the boat during its last two patrols of the war. Germerhausen was a fitting replacement—he was a bold attacker who preferred to get in a little closer than his predecessor. You'll note that most of his attacks were made from less than 2000 yards, and he fired smaller salvos of torpedoes.

On 27 May 1945, the Spadefish and crew set out from Guam for her 5th and final war patrol. She was accompanied by the USS Crevalle and the USS Sea Dog. This group was to be the first of a band that eventually grew to nine ships in the Sea of Japan.

The area had been inaccessible to American subs since 1942 after Japan placed mines across the narrow channels leading into their "backyard" sea. But because of successful minefield encounters elsewhere, Admiral Lockwood decided his subs were capable of making it through the minefields. Once inside the Sea of Japan, they would be able to sever the last trade lines to the Japanese Empire.

The first group made it safely through the southern entrance to the sea, the Tsushima Strait minefield, on 4 June. On each of the following two days, another group made a successful entry. With all nine subs safely through the minefield, everyone dispersed to patrol their assigned areas. They agreed not to fire on enemy shipping until after sunset on 9 June, to allow everyone to get into position before the enemy was aware of the incursion.

The Spadefish was assigned to work the northern end of the sea, just off the coast of Hokkaido Island. During her passage to the north, the watches spotted many freighters, all running straight and with running lights on at night. They seemed to be feeling perfectly secure. That would change over the next several days.

Torpedo Attack #1

Finally, dark came on 9 June. The Spadefish had been lying quietly outside of Ishikari Wan harbor, and now she slid silently into the harbor waters expecting to find it full of targets. The commander was disappointed to find nearly all of the ships inside the breakwater and out of reach. One ship was departing, but Germerhausen decided to let her go while he explored the area more. He eventually found a small freighter anchored with its running lights on. It looked like a perfect target. He lined her up for a straight shot from 1600 yards, and fired two torpedoes.

Both ran under the ship and missed. Captain Germerhausen decided to leave the small target and chase the ship seen departing earlier. He left the harbor at flank speed.

Torpedo Attack #2

The freighter was heavily loaded and traveling slowly. It took only an hour and a half to take up a good position off her flank. Germerhausen headed in to fire. At a range of 1350 yards, three torpedoes were fired on a straight track. All three hit and the ship disintegrated and sank in less than a minute. No sooner than that target settled into the sea, another appeared on radar, again the crew went to battle stations.

Torpedo Attack #3

This was another medium-sized freighter. It was heading into the harbor, and all the Spadefish had to do was sit and wait. She took up a perfect position off the freighter's track and fired three shots at a range of 2000 yards. Two hits were heard and observed and the target exploded and sank. The sub headed out to sea to clear the area and reload.

They had only been underway for about ten minutes when another target was picked up on radar.

Torpedo Attack #4

The Spadefish went to flank speed and closed on the unsuspecting target, another medium-sized freighter traveling alone.

They arrived at the firing position late and so had to shoot with a fairly large gyro angle. This proved to be no problem: Two of the three torpedoes fired from 1990 yards found their mark, and the ship broke in two and quickly sank. Feeling the ships had sunk rapidly enough to prevent them from sending a warning, Germerhausen decided to stay in the area for a submerged patrol at dawn.

During the day of 10 June, several ships were spotted, but they were too small and not worth attacking. The Spadefish continued to patrol quietly. Later that night, she surfaced for her night patrol and spotted a good-sized target on radar. The target's track was set and the sub started an end-around

Torpedo Attack #5

Captain Germerhausen couldn't get a good look at the target in the darkness, but she was acting very suspiciously. Just as he was about to fire from 1600 yards, the ship turned hard and headed straight for the Spadefish. Germerhausen ordered three torpedoes fired down-the-throat and he reversed course to evade the oncoming ship. The target closed to within 1300 yards and opened fire on the Spadefish. The torpedoes missed.

With the enemy gunners getting their mark and bullets flying on both sides of the boat, the commander took her deep. The crew rigged for depth charges and waited. The enemy passed overhead and in three minutes dropped 18 charges on the Spadefish, but she wasn't damaged. She continued west submerged.

Most of June 11 was spent out to sea getting a good battery charge and allowing the crew to have a much-deserved rest. The next morning, the sub headed back toward the coat of Hokkaido and spotted a good-sized motor sampan. Germerhausen ordered it destroyed with the deck gun, and later that morning, two trawlers were also demolished with fire from the deck gun.

Torpedo Attack #6

Early on the 13 June, two targets were picked up on radar just west of the La Perouse Strait on the northern tip of Hokkaido. Captain Germerhausen began tracking and found one target moving, and another lying to.

He headed after the moving ship and closed in for a flank attack. At a range of only 1300 yards, the captain ordered two torpedoes fired. Both hit. He immediately reversed course to line up the other ship, which still hadn't moved, and headed in at flank speed in an attempt to beat the coming dawn. Concerned about the nationality of the freighter, Captain Germerhausen closed to within 8000 yards and confirmed that it was a Russian freighter, so he left it unmolested. By the time the identity of the second ship was confirmed, the first had sunk.

Torpedo Attack #7

Just before dawn on 14 June, when the Spadefish was still patrolling just offshore, the watch spotted a promising target. Luck was with the crew of the sub—the ship was lying to. At 5000 yards, Captain Germerhausen got a good look and saw that it was a heavily loaded freighter. The captain brought the sub to within 2000 yards, and since he had four fish aft and only two forward, he swung around for a stern shot. He fired one torpedo at the center of the ship on a perfect 90-degree track. It hit, but the target didn't sink. He fired another on the same track. This one hit also. Captain Germerhausen watched as the target started to roll, and all lifeboats were deployed. Several minutes later, the target capsized and sank. The Spadefish headed out to sea and submerged to 150 feet to avoid the predictable air search, which could be expected with the morning light.

Germerhausen continued to patrol to the south for several days without seeing anything worthy of attack until just after midnight on 17 June, when the Spadefish made a good radar contact.

Torpedo Attack #8

The watch spotted three ships, and Captain Germerhausen ordered the crew to battle stations. After maneuvering for a good position, he fired the last two bow torpedoes at a medium freighter, the largest of the three ships. A gyro angle of zero was used from a range of 2100 yards—a perfect setup. One torpedo hit the target, and before the sub could set up for a stern shot, the ship sank.

Torpedo Attack #9

After dawn on 18 June, a small freighter came into view, and there was a brief scare when the Spadefish encountered what appeared to be a destroyer. When Germerhausen was certain the sub wasn't in danger, he closed to 1000 yards and fired one stern torpedo at the freighter. The torpedo ran straight and true but passed under the light freighter. The last shot was fired, set to run shallower. It, too, passed right under the ship.

After patrolling the area for several days in search of targets that could be sunk with the gun, the Spadefish finally gave up and headed north through the La Perouse Strait, and home.

Although the commander claimed a total tonnage sunk of over 28,000 tons, postwar investigations only gave him credit for 10,000 tons. He was given credit for five ships and several smaller sampans.

While the Spadefish was being readied for another patrol in the Sea of Japan, peace arrived. A few weeks later, she steamed home to Mare Island with a marvelous war record: Decorated with the highest award—the Presidential Unit Citation—and four Battle Stars, she had conducted five successful war patrols without a single casualty, and fired 78 torpedoes, resulting in 53 hits—a truly outstanding achievement.

By directive dated January 1947, the USS Spadefish was placed out of commission at Mare Island.

28 USS Parche 2nd Patrol

One of the most daring and exciting attacks of the war was turned in by the Parche during her second patrol near Formosa. It was certainly the closest in terms of range to the enemy—the combatants were frequently within rock-throwing range of each other.

The Parche was part of a three-ship wolf pack. The other ships in the pack were the Steelhead and the Hammerhead. Transit to the patrol area was quiet, and the patrol was rather unproductive until the evening of 4 July when Commander "Red" Ramage took the boat in on the surface to attack a group of ships. Upon closer inspection, the ships turned out to be destroyers and cruisers. As Captain Ramage turned and made full speed away, the Japanese provided and impressive fireworks display.

Captain Ramage battled bad weather and equipment problems for the remainder of the month until he received a contact report from the Hammerhead: A large convoy was heading his way. After chasing the radically maneuvering convoy for several hours, it finally showed on radar just after midnight. He took an approach course and closed in.

By 0330, he was close enough to make out the convoy and its escorts. It was then that one of the escorts headed for the submarine at full speed. The Parche was also moving at full speed. Captain Ramage made a hard turn to the rear of the group, which placed him suddenly between the escorts and the convoy. The range was closing fast. A large freighter was in good position, but by the time he could set up, the range was only 450 yards—too close to fire torpedoes.

He turned hard and pulled out of the freighter's path, missing by a scant 200 yards. He continued to turn and, once clear, fired two torpedoes, but the ship had been alerted and swung hard to avoid them. This hard turn effectively cut off one of the escorts coming after the Parche, so Captain Ramage continued the attack.

Two large tankers appeared off to starboard, and Ramage headed for them, still on the surface. A five-minute run at high speed brought the tankers in range. He opened fire from 1500 yards. All four torpedoes hit the first tanker along the side—it sank almost immediately, leaving only a burning oil slick on the surface.

The Parch came hard right again to bring the stern tubes to bear on the second tanker, and fired three torpedoes. Two hit home. The target slowed but didn't stop, and the Parche continued at high speed, as the men below hurried to reload the empty tubes.

The escorts were becoming a problem—firing guns and flares indiscriminately—but another ship appeared as Ramage received word that two torpedoes were ready forward. From 800 yards, he fired both, resulting in two hits. Struck squarely amidships, the target sank in minutes.

Ramage came right to avoid an oncoming escort and headed back toward the second tanker. The Parche crossed about 200 yards behind it and opened up for a stern shot. At 800 yards, Ramage fired three stern tubes at the tanker. All hit. Having taken five torpedo hits, the tanker went down, leaving only another oily fire behind on the surface.

Although they had already taken two ships, the real prize of the group was a large freighter. Ramage was turning to attack it when a small, fast ship was seen heading straight for the Parche, intent on ramming. Ramage called below for the engineers to pour on all the oil they had. "The other fellow had the right of way, but we were in a hurry." When halfway across the escort's bow, Ramage put the rudder full to the right and swung the stern clear at the last second. The Japanese were "screaming . . . as we cleared by less than 50 feet. Mutual cheers and jeers were exchanged by all hands."

Ramage then found himself boxed in on both sides by smaller craft and had the large freighter dead ahead with a zero angle on the bow. There was nothing for him to do but try a down-the-throat shot. The first fish was away but it veered to the right, so he calmly recalculated the solution, and fired two more. Those two hit, stopping the freighter dead in her tracks. The Parche passed down the side of the damaged ship and then turned away to bring the stern tubes around. From 800 yards, Captain Ramage fired one torpedo. It was a bull's-eye, hitting right in the middle of the ship.

Ramage took a moment to look around while still on the surface. The injured freighter was down by the nose and as Ramage headed back for the coup de grace, the target's stern came up and she made a nose dive for the bottom.

With no large targets left and the gyro-setting device in the forward torpedo room jammed, Ramage wisely decided to put some distance between "us and this hornet's nest." Several explosions were seen as the Parche pulled away—it was Steelhead's turn to get in her blows.

Almost out of torpedoes and with a pharmacist's mate suffering from acute appendicitis, the Parche headed for home.

29 USS Ray 5th Patrol

The Ray was one of the many fine ships to come out of the shipyard at Manitowoc, Wisconsin. She was tested and conducted her first training maneuvers in the waters of Lake Michigan. On 9 July 1944, she departed Fremantle, Australia for her 5th war patrol. In charge was Commander William T. Kinsella.

Torpedo Attack #1

After conducting training exercises for several days, the Ray headed toward the Lombok Strait to patrol. Sighting nothing but patrol craft in the straits, Captain Kinsella headed into the Java Sea and quickly located a fully loaded tanker with no escort. He pushed the sub to all-ahead flank and made an end-around maneuver.

He made his approach on the surface in the dark. At a range of 3000 yards, Captain Kinsella fired all six forward tubes. Three hits were scored: torpedoes 1, 2, and 4. The tanker was struck in the bow, under the bridge, and MOT (Middle Of Target). The target seemed to shake off the damage and continue on course at the same speed.

A hard turn brought the stern tubes to bear, and all four tubes were fired. The target slowed as the torpedoes were fired, and all missed ahead of the ship. Both torpedo rooms worked furiously to reload. When three fish were loaded forward, the captain again gave the fire order. Three torpedoes were fired at the target, which had now stopped—range 2900 yards. Shots one and two took an unexplained jig to the left and missed. Number three hit in the bow. He ordered another turn for the stern tubes. Once again, all four torpedoes were set to fire, but as Kinsella was about to shoot, the tanker fired at the sub. The first shot was very close and the captain ordered flank speed to start maneuvering. During this process, all four stern tubes were emptied with no hits.

By now Captain Kinsella had been at this enterprise for almost two hours, and had expended 17 torpedoes, but he was determined. The tubes were reloaded again. Dawn was approaching as the Ray made a submerged attack, and three forward torpedoes were fired when the light was good enough to see through the scope. Two hits. Still the tanker remained afloat! Two more forward torpedoes were fired from 1800 yards, and both hit under the stack. Finally, at about 0700, the tanker started to sink and the Ray went deep to clear the area.

With 22 torpedoes gone, Captain Kinsella decided to return to Fremantle and reload. On July 28, the Ray once again departed Fremantle and headed north. Back in the Lombok Straits, Captain Kinsella tracked what appeared to be a ship. When it suddenly dropped off the radar screen, he realized it must have been a submarine, and the Ray quickly left the area.

Torpedo Attack #2

The Ray crossed the Java Sea to patrol the southern entrance to the Makassar Strait. At 0330 in the morning on 14 August, the watch spotted a slow-moving two-ship convoy. Close inspection showed one freighter and fired four shots, resulting in three hits. The freighter broke in two and sank quickly. The escort poured on the coal and headed for the Ray, but thanks to the MK 18 wakeless torpedoes, the escort captain couldn't get a fix on the Ray's position. He dropped his charges well off the mark.

Torpedo Attack #3

Several days of patrolling the southern and western coast of Borneo proved unproductive. As the Ray moved toward the Natuna Islands, the watch spotted smoke on the horizon. A large convoy appeared to be headed toward the sub.

Captain Kinsella tracked the convoy until he had a good fix on its course and destination. It appeared to be going to Miri on the northern coast of Malaysia. The convoy was receiving air cover, so a daytime attack was postponed. Knowing the convoy's course, Captain Kinsella moved ahead and waited for dark. As the convoy approached by night, the captain could finally get a good look at it. There were 12 ships, five of which were escorts. About midnight, he slid behind an outlying escort. A small turn brought the stern tubes to bear and four shots were fired. Kinsella watched amazed as all missed. The setup had been perfect; all that the could imagine was that the boat's wake had somehow thrown the fish off course. He immediately went to flank speed and cleared the area.

Once safely away, he made another end-around. At 0100, he again slipped behind one of the escorts, but this time kept on going toward the convoy. He chose a large tanker for the target and all six forward torpedoes were fired from 4000 yards. If they had approached any closer, the Ray would have been surrounded by escorts. Once the torpedoes were fired, the Ray made a hard turn in front of another escort and headed back out.

The first torpedo hit one of the freighters overlapping the tanker. Three more hit the tanker which erupted with "one of the most terrific explosions I've ever seen," according to the captain. He continued to track the convoy by radar as the Ray left the area, and he watched the freighter and tanker drop off the radar screen as they sank.

Torpedo Attack #4

The Ray proceeded up the coast, and on 18 August, the watch spotted a plane circling over smoke, a sign of a convoy.

The convoy consisted of at least 12 ships, 5 of which were tankers. The Ray ran at 120 feet during the approach to avoid being spotted from the air. Once under the escort screen, Captain Kinsella came up to periscope depth for six quick shots. A large tanker took three hits and a smaller freighter took another. The Ray headed for 370 feet at flank speed. On its way down, the crew heard the tanker sink. They found a thermal layer at 170 feet, and under it, the Ray easily avoided the escorts. Once the sub was in the clear, Captain Kinsella surfaced and began to chase again.

Torpedo Attack #5

Several days of chasing the convoy led the USS Ray to a chance meeting with the submarine USS Harder. The captains exchanged information and decided to attack the convoy, which was now just outside of Paluan Bay, at dawn.

The next morning, the Ray moved into position. The crew heard what seemed to be torpedo explosions from the Harder, and the convoy started moving toward the Ray. As the group came by, Kinsela fired his last four torpedoes at a large freighter. One good hit exploded the boiler of the freighter, and the crew could hear the freighter breaking up as they headed deep.

A heavy depth charge attack drove the Ray down to 425 feet, with no thermal layer to hide under. Two hours later, Captain Kinsella managed to take the sub back up to periscope depth for a look around. The target had sunk and the convoy had moved on. A lone escort circled the area looking for survivors. The Ray cleared the area submerged and headed for Fremantle.

30 USS Ray 6th Patrol

The Ray's 6th war patrol began on 23 September 1944, when she set sail from Fremantle for the South China Sea. The crew conducted training while making passage up through the Lombok and Makassar Straits.

Once in the Celebes Sea, the watch sighted a well-built sailboat. The captain decided to attack with guns. He surfaced and ordered the crew to clear the decks with fire from the two 20mm machine guns and then finish the ship off with the four-inch deck gun. They approached to close range and the order to fire was given. Both guns jammed. They headed back out and managed to get the rear gun cleared and once again were ordered to fire. This time, the firing pin broke. By this time also, the ship was sending up flares and causing quite a commotion. The captain decided to give up the whole thing. He noted in his report that they would "stick to shooting torpedoes."

They continued through the Celebes Sea and through the Sibutu Passage into the Sulu Sea and the Philippine area.

Torpedo Attack #1

In the early evening on 6 October, the sub began tracking a large tanker with two destroyer escorts. The captain put on all four engines and moved ahead of the target. Once in position, he closed the range to shoot.

As he was moving in, a destroyer turned toward the sub. Captain Kinsella didn't think the Ray had been spotted, but he decided not to question an approaching destroyer, so, at an extreme range of 4200 yards, he fired six torpedoes at the tanker.

Moving away on the surface, he saw only one hit. A flaw in the target-bearing transmitter fouled up the firing solution, and another end-around put the sub too close to an escort, so they were forced to go deep.

A third end-around put the sub in another questionable firing position, but Captain Kinsella took the chance and fired six more shots. Three torpedoes were heard to hit and again the sub was forced under by the escorts. The tanker was spotted the next day, smoking but still afloat.

Things continued on a sour note as Captain Kinsella tracked a destroyer for several days but was unable to close on it.

Torpedo Attack #2

Finally, on 12 October, Kinsella's luck changed as a large freighter with two escorts steamed into view. He drove in as the escorts conveniently moved aside to give a clear shot. Four forward torpedoes were fired: Two hit with rocking explosions and the freighter was literally blown to pieces.

The two escorts caused trouble for several hours before the Ray was able to return to periscope depth. Almost immediately, Captain Kinsella started tracking more smoke. When he closed in, he was disappointed to find that the smoke was from the boilers of the two destroyers looking for him! The Ray quietly moved away.

The next day, problems arose when the sub dove to avoid a Japanese plane in the area. As the boat slid under the waves, the captain realized he hadn't heard the report that the hatch was closed or felt the pressure in the boat. He immediately dropped through the hatch to the control room as the water poured through the conning tower hatch. The hatch had been pulled to, but not secured.

The boat went down to 80 feet before it could be brought under control and retuned to the surface. The hatch to the conning tower had been closed leaving the executive officer and several others trapped. Back on the surface, the captain went up through the engine room hatch and then up to the conning tower.

When he opened the hatch, he was greeted by several happy crewman who informed him that the topside crew was all right but the conning tower was two-thirds flooded. Pumps were put to work to remove the water, but most of the electronics were damaged by the salt water bath. The damage couldn't be repaired at sea, so a quick trip to Biak, in New Guinea, was ordered for repairs.

Torpedo Attack #3

After a remarkable refit-and-repair job by the USS Orion, the Ray was back on patrol, and on 1 November, the crew was back at battle stations.

A large convoy had been spotted in the Mindoro Strait and Captain Kinsella closed in for a shot. The largest ship was a freighter; there were also four small tankers. He lined up the freighter, but before he could shoot, it was hit by another sub's torpedoes. The attack team in the Ray started looking for other targets. Soon the tankers turned away from the other sub and toward the Ray.

The closer the tankers came, the better they looked. As two of the tankers were overlapping at 900 yards, Captain Kinsella fired three aft torpedoes. The first ship took two hits and blew up, sending oil drums flying high into the air. The second took one hit and stopped dead in the water. Both sank as the Ray was heading for deep water.

A good thermal layer hid the sub well as it moved out of the area.

Torpedo Attack #4

Several days later, the sub had moved north to the Lingayen Gulf area and spotted a burning transport ship. A closer look showed that the superstructure was well ablaze but the hull was intact. It had probably been bomb from the air.

Ray moved in to finish the job. Two well-aimed torpedoes sent it to the bottom in a matter of minutes, but then a shore-based radar appeared to have picked up the sub—an escort was moving toward it. Rapid withdrawal was in order.

Torpedo Attack #5

On 6 November, when the Ray was patrolling off Cape Bolinao, a wild battle occurred when several subs closed in on a convoy at once. Explosions were heard as the Ray moved in at 120 feet. As Captain Kinsella was lining up a

Japanese cruiser for a shot, torpedoes passed the Ray on the port side and then again to starboard. The target cruiser reversed course.

As the ship once again showed her side to the Ray, Captain Kinsella fired four torpedoes and went deep. It was a madhouse of activity. Torpedoes from several subs were flying about, bombs were being dropped by aircraft, and depth charges were exploding all at once. Two good hits blew the bow off of the cruiser, but it didn't sink.

Escorts kept the Ray deep for a while, and while he was waiting, Captain Kinsella decided to move to the shore side of the convoy for another attack. While moving at 370 feet, he lightly grounded the boat. It was an easy job to back her off the bottom, but the forward sound head had been rubbed off and the cable blew back into the forward room causing a rapid leak.

The sub had to move back up to periscope depth so the crew could stop the leak with a wooden plug. A tanker was sighted taking the cruiser in tow, and the captain was heartbroken to watch the cruiser being towed off. He had a perfect shot at it, but to fire a torpedo would have been suicide—escorts were only 800 yards away and the plug in the forward room prevented a deep dive. He returned after dark to look for the cruiser on the surface, but it was nowhere to be found.

Torpedo Attack #6

Several days of repair activity and patrolling climaxed with a contact report from the USS Raton. Captain Kinsella poured on the oil and headed toward the contact area. Around dark, the sub made contact and prepared for a night surface attack. The Ray approached slowly in the darkness and watched the convoy's zig pattern.

A nice zig toward the sub put the second ship in a good firing position, and Captain Kinsella quickly took advantage of it. With several other subs tracking the same group of ships, the captain wanted to be sure he came away with something. The order was given to fire all six forward tubes at the target freighter.

Four hits completely disintegrated the ship with such a flash that Kinsella took the boat down for fear of being spotted. Shortly after, another torpedo was heard to hit. The Ray had "gotten lucky"—an escort on the far side of the convoy was hit. More explosions were heard, and when Captain Kinsella returned to the surface, he received word that there were no more targets left.

The Ray headed out to the east, and several days later, its last two torpedoes were fired at a ship grounded on a shallow reef. Both missed due to strong currents. Captain Kinsella pointed the bow towards Midway.

31 USS Rasher 5th Patrol

The USS Rasher saw success nearly every time she left port. For her highly profitable 1st, 3rd, 4th, and 5th patrols, she was awarded the Presidential Unit Citation. Her 5th patrol was particularly remarkable.

After an excellent refit at Fremantle, Australia, the Rasher set out on her 5th war patrol on 22 July 1944. Commander Henry G. Munson had just taken over and was in for the ride of his life. Rasher headed north through the Lombok Strait and toward the patrol area just off Luzon.

Torpedo Attack #1

The Commander's first attack with the Rasher was on 6 August. A radar contact developed into a Japanese convoy. There were one large freighter, two smaller freighters, and two escorts. The Rasher approached on the flank and fired six torpedoes at the large freighter. Captain Munson was forced deep to avoid being rammed by one of the smaller ships. Five hits were heard along with the noises of a ship breaking up and sinking.

Lifeguard duty and tropical storms were the order of the day until 18 August when another convoy was spotted. This one was a major movement of at least 13 ships.

Torpedo Attack #2

Due to the extreme darkness, Captain Munson had to rely on radar information; therefore, the exact composition of the group was undetermined.

Around 2100, he moved in and fired two aft torpedoes at a large target. Unsure of the gyro settings, he pulled out to recheck the situation. The setup must have been good, however, because both shots hit home, causing a huge explosion and fire. The target must have been a large, loaded tanker. The bow of the ship blew off and landed 500 yards away. Both pieces burned fiercely for a moment and then disappeared.

The escorts started firing wildly into the night. Tracers were flying in all directions and depth charges were being dropped rapidly. The sight was spectacular, but the captain was busy planning his next attack.

Torpedo Attack #3

The Rasher moved ahead of the convoy and waited. The convoy took a slight zig and improved the Rasher's position. When the targets lined up again, six forward torpedoes were fired at one large target. The stern was swung around and four more fish were fired at a second target.

The first ship took three hits and started to burn. The second ship took three hits, and a lucky fourth hit was heard on a ship beyond the targets. The second ship was believed to be another large tanker—a huge oil slick was spotted later at its last known position, which indicated that it too had sunk.

Then an escort sighted the Rasher, and she had to pull away from the convoy to shake it off her tail. The first target, a large transport, was seen falling behind the group, but eventually it disappeared from radar.

The captain now pulled away from the group and called for help—he was almost out of torpedoes and there were still many large targets in the area. He hoped to get several other boats in on the action, as the convoy was breaking up into several groups and he couldn't track them all.

Torpedo Attack #4

Munson tracked the largest of the groups, and with all remaining torpedoes loaded, he moved in again. Four bow torpedoes were fired at the leading ship. Rasher swung around to fire two stern shots at the second ship; both were large targets. Three hits were seen on the first ship and the fourth was another lucky hit on a ship beyond the target. Two torpedoes ripped into the second target. The first target stopped in her tracks and, after several large explosions, she sank.

The Rasher was now completely out of torpedoes, but she stayed in the area to guide the USS Bluefish and the USS Spadefish to profitable targets. After a period of such long and furious activity, the crew was thankful for a rest. They headed north up through the Balintang Channel and on to Midway.

The masterful shooting of Munson and crew vaulted them close to the top of the list for tonnage sunk in a single patrol. Munson initially claimed five ships for 45,700 tons, but later investigation and interviews with POWs showed that one of the targets sunk on that dark, overcast night was a 20,000-ton aircraft carrier, so they raised his official total to 52,600 tons—quite a night!

32 USS Cabrilla 6th Patrol

Many of the Cabrilla's eight patrols weren't normal anti-shipping sweeps, but instead, special missions. She delivered and picked up island guerrillas, laid mines, and made photo reconnaissance deep into enemy waters. These missions were very important but limited her time spent hunting ships, and thus kept her overall total down. But when given the chance, the Cabrilla showed herself to be a true hunter. She was given such a chance on her 6th patrol, and in one week, sank four of the seven ships she would sink for the entire war.

The Cabrilla and crew left Fremantle on 13 September 1944 under the command of Lt. Commander W.C. Thompson. The sub headed north through the Lombok Strait and on up toward the Philippines, passing through the Sibutu Passage on 23 September.

The first shipping contact came the next day as the watch sighted a large, loosely formed convoy. Captain Thompson attempted to approach submerged but couldn't gain a suitable position. After tracking the convoy's course, it was obvious they couldn't catch it before it reached safety in Manila, so they broke off the attack.

Torpedo Attack #1

On 1 October, a better opportunity presented itself: Sonar picked up echo-ranging of a destroyer at 0919, and Captain Thompson turned to investigate. Smoke was sighted on the horizon at 0942, and a convoy was in sight by 1017. There were three tankers, several smaller freighters, and two escorts. They moved ahead to try to slip past the escort to the side of the convoy. All the ships zigged toward them, but the Cabrilla didn't appear to have a good contact.

The crew all held their breath as the escort passed 50 yards to port; the captain took a quick look with the periscope and saw nothing but gray paint! In the meantime, the convoy had made a zig away and the largest tanker was now in a bad position for attack. The crew switched setup to a freighter and fired four bow torpedoes for three hits. The ship blew up and sank in pieces. The other two bow torpedoes were fired at another tanker, resulting in a hit.

The escort was now approaching from the rear. Since there were no other good target for a stern shot, Captain Thompson fired four torpedoes down-the-throat at the escort. He thought one hit but couldn't confirm what he heard—depth charges were being dropped in the distance. The arrival of a Nell bomber caused him to break off the attack and remain submerged for the rest of the day.

Torpedo Attack #2

After lunchtime on 6 September, a large convoy came right down the track the Cabrilla. Very little maneuvering was needed, which was good, since the Cabrilla had developed a shaft squeak that would limit its ability to move quietly. Several cargo ships were about to overlap, so Thompson held his fire. When the two ships made one large target, he fired all six forward torpedoes from 1800 yards. Five were heard to hit as he headed for deep water—three on one ship and two on another. Loud breaking-up noises were heard from two different directions. A good temperature gradient was found at 380 feet where the Cabrilla sat out the 36 depth charges that came looking for her.

Torpedo Attack #3

That night, two destroyers showed up on radar. They were looking for the U.S. sub. A quick setup was made and all six forward tubes were emptied. The destroyers zigged at the right moment and all the torpedoes missed. Thompson quickly turned the boat to use the stern tubes. All four tubes were fired from 3100 yards, and again all missed. The destroyers didn't even know they had been fired upon as they continued on their way.

Torpedo Attack #4

At 0300 the next morning, Captain Thompson received a contact report from the USS Aspro, which was also in the area. He poured on the speed to close the estimated convoy track. A lone freighter came over the hill and they started to track it. He submerged at 11,000 yards in broad daylight at 0546. There didn't seem to be a destroyer escort, so Thompson continued to approach, even with the noisy shaft. The lone ship continued. At a range of 1400 yards, Captain Thompson fired the last four bow torpedoes: Three were hits and the target broke in half. The captain watched through the scope as the ship sank in a matter of seconds.

Now out of torpedoes, the Cabrilla headed for Pearl.

33 USS Hammerhead 2nd Patrol

The Hammerhead was unfortunate to come along rather late in the war—it saw limited duty. Captain Martin and his crew, however, took full advantage of what time they had. The best performance was turned in during the Hammerhead's 2nd patrol. She left Fremantle on 9 September 1944 bound to patrol the Java Sea and the Lombok and Makassar Straits.

Once in the Java Sea, the captain tried to make his crossing on the surface at night and under water during the day. One evening, while the sub was traveling on the surface, something appeared on the radar. Unable to identify it as a ship or island, Captain Martin ordered the boat to submerge. As he was passing through 60 feet of water, the captain received a dreaded call from the conning tower: "I think we left a man topside, Captain." A quick nose count proved the officer to be wrong, but only after several very tense minutes.

Several days of patrolling suspected shipping lanes yielded few contacts and no good torpedo targets. The Hammerhead continued to move slowly, and on 1 October, the watch finally sighted a convoy. Captain Martin began to close.

Torpedo Attack #1

The convoy was heading straight toward the sub. The Hammerhead pulled away a bit and then headed back in on the convoy's flank. When the lead ship of the five-ship group was at a range of 5500 yards and showing an angle on the bow of 60 degrees, the captain turned and headed for it.

At a range of 3800 yards, he fired three forward torpedoes at the lead freighter. The second freighter was overlapping behind the first, so the captain hoped one of the three shots at the first target might hit the second. He fired three torpedoes at the third target and started to swing around to use the stern tubes. The first two torpedoes hit on time and all bridge personnel saw a huge flame shoot up as the first target exploded. A very bright orange explosion was seen as the forth torpedo hit the third ship, which also blew up.

He fired two fish each at a medium freighter and a small tanker. He saw one hit the freighter and two hit the tanker. The Hammerhead was having quite a night. As the two ships attempted to escape, a large white cloud poured out over the water. The freighter sank first, followed later by the tanker. The second ship and three escorts continued to steam on.

The captain pulled away and made a quick run around an island to try to gain a firing position on the remaining ship, but he couldn't regain contact and decided to make for deeper water.

Several quiet weeks passed as the ship made routine patrols, avoided minefields, and dodged surface debris. Then, early in the morning of 21 October, a six-ship convoy came into contact and the crew of the Hammerhead went to battle stations.

The target base course was 200 degrees with irregular 20 degree zigs. The starboard side of the group seemed to be the least defended by escorts, so Captain Martin decided to attack there. While the Hammerhead maneuvered in on the starboard flank, the lone escort refused to play ball. It moved into the approach path and continued to close, so the captain turned his tail to it and pulled away behind the thick smoke produced by the engines on full power. The escort apparently thought it had a false contact and didn't follow.

The sub made a turn and headed back in for another attempt. This time the escort let the sub slip behind her, but quarters were very close. As the sub steadied to fire, the escort fired as well. The target ships were bunched very closely together so they fired all six forward torpedoes with a wide spread, hoping to hit something. The Hammerhead then turned and poured on the fuel to get away from the escort. Shortly thereafter, two hits were heard from the convoy. The escort continued to fire, but the gun crew was shooting behind the sub at the smoke cloud.

With the range to the escort only 1400 yards, Captain Martin decided to try a down-the-throat shot from the stern tubes. Two fish were sent away at zero-gyro angles. They were heard to explode, but the escort was undamaged, so they must have exploded prematurely or hit one of the many floating logs in the area.

Probably afraid to get too far from the rest of the convoy, the escort turned back. Two large explosions garnered the attention of the bridge crew on the Hammerhead, and they turned to see the last two ships in the group break out in flames and start to fall back. At 8000 yards, one of the ships disappeared, and several minutes later, the other vanished in an explosion.

Not satisfied, the Hammerhead continued to track the group, and at 0320 headed back in for another shot. At 4500 yards Captain Martin fired again at a large target showing a nice 95-degree angle on the bow. Two explosions were seen and the target went under in less than a minute. The escorts started firing all around but couldn't pick up the Hammerhead in the darkness. The sub slowly pulled away from the remaining escorts. With his boat low on torpedoes and uncomfortably close to several airfields, Captain Martin decided to leave the area before dawn.

Late that night he received a dispatch ordering the Hammerhead back to Fremantle.

34 USS Atule 1st Patrol

The captain and crew of the USS Atule probably knew the war was coming to a close when they left on their first war patrol in October of 1944. With time short, they must make their mark in a hurry. In four war patrols, the Atule scored an official six sinkings. Four of these were sunk on the Atule's 1st patrol under the command of J.H. Maurer.

The Atule set out from Pearl Harbor on 9 October 1944 bound for the Luzon straits, South China Sea area. Training and tracking practice were the crew's first order of business. It was a good thing they encountered few enemy ships during their first few weeks at sea—they had a chance to master every drill and procedure. Actually, the crew ran into many more U.S. subs during its transit than it did enemy ships: At least a half-dozen American submersibles were sighted or contacted.

The first good ship contact came on 25 October, but as they maneuvered to close the range, three explosions were heard as a pack mate, the USS Jallao, arrived there first.

Torpedo Attack #1

On 1 November, the Atule's luck improved: At 0331 the watch sighted a freighter moving with two escorts. The moon was full and there were broken clouds as the Atule maneuvered around several rain squalls, trying to stay hidden. Several radical zigs put the captain in a position to attack if he acted quickly. At 5600 yards, he decided it was now or never. He turned to head toward the target, keeping his bow pointed at the near escort. At 1550 yards, he fired all six forward torpedoes at what now appeared to be a large troop transport.

A huge explosion resulted from the first torpedo hit and Captain Maurer ordered the Atule down. As the boat was submerging, he heard two more hits, followed by the usual breaking-up noises of a sinking ship. By noon the next day, they were back in the area to take a look at the scene. There was a lot of debris and a single destroyer was still in the area, but there was no sign of the target ship except for a large oil slick.

The Atule cleared the area to patrol in the Hong Kong to Manila traffic lane. On 3 November, the Atule received a contact report from pack mate Jallao regarding a five-ship convoy. Again, she arrived just in time to see others make the attack.

More disappointment was in store on 13 November as the sub tried to close on a carrier group they sighted, but after chasing on the surface all night, they were forced to give it up when dawn arrived with the threat of patrol aircraft. Once submerged, the captain knew he would never catch the group. The ships were making 20 knots—easy enough to accomplish on the surface but impossible under water. It was heart-breaking to watch the huge target move over the hill and out of sight.

Torpedo Attack #2

More slow days followed until 20 November, when radar picked up a promising target. The captain made all speed ahead and pulled in front of the target and waited. Soon a destroyer steamed into view and Captain Maurer took aim. Three torpedoes were fired from 2500 yards for one hit, but it was enough. Two and a half minutes later, the destroyer's stern stood straight up and slid under. The sub cleared the area and headed west.

Torpedo Attack #3

On 24 November, a group of ships that had eluded the Atule the day before suddenly appeared, heading straight for the sub. The captain moved around the group after the moon set, in order to attack with a black cloud at his back.

He moved in on the starboard bow of a large transport ship but drew to a stop as an escort came into view at 2000 yards. He kept the bow pointed toward the escort and "perspired freely." Maurer held fire until the escort was overlapping with the transport and then fired all six forward tubes. The first two hit the destroyer and the third hit the transport.

The Atule went flank speed ahead into a turn, bringing the stern tubes into play. Two more shots were fired at the transport. The destroyer suddenly exploded, shaking the boat "like a terrier shaking a rat," and all that remained of it was oil burning on the water.

The transport took another hit, and the Atule moved away to open the range as the other escort opened up with sporadic bursts of gunfire. At a range of 11,000 yards, they saw the transport sink.

Torpedo Attack #4

Early in the morning on 27 November, the Atule made radar contact with a target making radical zigs. The night was bright, and with the brightest part of the sky behind them, they had to approach with caution. This original contact was lost, but the maneuvering put them into position to locate a pip on the radar between two islands.

As they moved closer, it became obvious that the target was an anchored ship—an easy target. The Atule circled to the west to get a good background for the approach. Radar couldn't pick the ship up due to the land behind it, so the captain moved in close enough to make out the range with binoculars. At 2000 yards, he fired four bow torpedoes and watched as hits spread along the entire length of the ship. The ship burned like a torch. Its flames were still visible from 15 miles away as the Atule made for deep water.

The next day the captain headed for home.

35 USS Flasher 5th Patrol

No list of great patrols would be complete without mention of the Flasher's 5th patrol, the famous "Great Tanker Shoot." She was already a veteran of three successful patrols when she left Fremantle on 15 November 1944 for her 5th patrol.

As usual, the first days at sea were uneventful as the boat moved north through the Makassar Strait, Sibutu Pass, and the Mindoro Strait into the South China Sea. Plane contacts began on 23 November and kept the crew on its toes, but nothing worth attacking came into view until 4 December.

Captain Grider received a contact report on a west-bound convoy, and soon discovered that he was right in the path of the group. Shortly after, the convoy appeared. Amidst low visibility and frequent rain squalls, the Flasher began tracking from ahead of the convoy.

Torpedo Attack #1

Large swells made depth control a problem, and visibility was very poor; the watch could only get an occasional glimpse of a mast top. Then, as the Flasher closed to 8000 yards, the entire convoy was blocked from sight by a downpour.

At 2000 yards, a destroyer popped out of the mist and steamed into firing position. At 0915, the captain ordered four torpedoes fired on gyro angles between 28 and 51 at a range of 1600 yards The first two hit, stopping the target dead in the water. She was settling by the stern as Captain Grier turned his attention to a large tanker.

He set up a stern shot, and at 0918, fired the first torpedo. He had a depth-control problem. The periscope went under the surface and wouldn't come back out. A second torpedo was fired without a spread. When the scope could clear the surface again, the tanker was turning. Captain Grier checked his fire. A quick look at the damaged destroyer showed it still afloat, it also revealed another escort heading straight for them at less than 1000 yards. Grider went deep in a hurry, and as the sub dove, he heard two timed hits on the tanker. He realized he must have underestimated her speed: The turn slowed her enough to catch two fish in the stern. "Verily, we smell of the rose."

A severe depth charge attack followed, with too many close calls. Captain Grider slipped beneath a temperature gradient and moved away to reload.

Torpedo Attack #2

With tubes reloaded, the Flasher headed back to the tanker, which was now ablaze. The first destroyer had sunk, but another took its place. Grider planned to attack this destroyer and finish off the tanker. A rain squall moved in and, once again, it was difficult for him to see.

A shape appeared up ahead, on the move, so he tracked it for a while before determining it was an escort ship. He turned back in and found the destroyer still stopped near the tanker. Four torpedoes were fired for hits and the destroyer was blown apart. Again, a hard depth charging followed, lasting 29 minutes. The Flasher surfaced later to see the tanker now burning from end to end and sure to sink. It had been totally abandoned, so the captain cleared the area.

Several frustrating weeks followed this fast start. The Flasher was plagued by patrol planes and high seas, and no more attacks were made until 22 December.

Torpedo Attack #3

Spirits were starting to droop on 22 December until the early morning radar operator reported that what he thought were the Tortuga Islands now appeared to be underway!

The "Tortugas" turned out to be a convoy spotted the day before but beyond attack. The tracking party went to work, and the sub worked ahead of the convoy. A destroyer remained in perfect position between the sub and the nearest ship, and several other escorts were seen, at the seaward side of the convoy. Realizing the best opportunity for attack was from the shore side, Commander Grider moved his boat into position. The convoy seemed to be composed of three large tankers.

At 0446, he moved in and fired three torpedoes at each of the first two tankers, range 2500 yards. A hard swing to the right brought the stern tubes around. Each of the first two tankers took two hits. Four stern shots were fired at the third tanker. Just after firing, the second tanker blew up, illuminating the area like a "night football game." The third tanker exploded immediately when hit, making visibility even better.

Flames from the second and third tankers flowed together to make a very impressive fire. Hoping to avoid a depth charge attack in such shallow water, Captain Grier moved off at flank speed plus. A few minutes later, the first ship blew up and added to the floating inferno. All hands had a chance to come topside to view the string of burning tankers. The crew heard explosions as all three tankers were swallowed by the flames and never seen again. Quite a good day's work.

The Flasher avoided several patrol boats and easily made it back to Australia, arriving on 30 December in fine shape.

36 USS Tirante 1st Patrol

The USS Tirante departed from Pearl Harbor on 3 March 1945 on her first war patrol. Even in 1945, the shipyards in New London, Connecticut continued to turn out new subs. The new boat was placed under Lt. Commander G. Street III. Serving as his executive officer was Lt. Commander Edward L. Beach, who later wrote several classic war novels, including *Run Silent, Run Deep*.

With a very experienced officer corps, the much younger crewmen were quickly trained, and on 25 March, they sailed quietly into Japanese waters.

Torpedo Attack #1

In the early afternoon on 25 March, a small freighter was seen on radar just south of the Japanese island of Kyushu. Captain Street made a submerged approach, and at 1340, three torpedoes were fired. The range was only 1000 yards and the run was a short one minute ten seconds. The crew was rewarded, after the short wait, with a tremendous explosion. The freighter had taken one hit and sank by the bow a minute later.

From there, the sub patrolled the area south of Kyushu and on up through the Tsushima Strait.

Torpedo Attack #2

While still in the strait, another ship was sighted as a possible target. The source of smoke turned out to be another small freighter. Street made his approach from the land side of the ship, and at a range of only 900 yards, he launched three torpedoes. The spread was one for the bow, one for the stern and one MOT (Middle of Target). One hit was recorded in the MOT, and the ship sank instantly. The captain noted proudly that the torpedo which hit was donated to the U.S. Navy by the workers at the Westinghouse MK 18 torpedo factory in Sharon, Pennsylvania. Their efforts were certainly rewarded.

Several local small sub hunters responded with a short salvo of depth charges, but none were close. The Tirante headed out of the area to let things cool off.

Gun Attack #1

Tirante spent a day or so on lifeguard duty for U.S. bombers attacking Kyushu. A small intercoastal ship appeared, and since it was unescorted, Captain Street decided it was a fitting gun target. Street ordered a battle surface gun, and they headed up. Several well-placed rounds brought the ship to a halt, and several more set it ablaze. The Tirante moved in close to take possible POWs, when a Japanese plane suddenly appeared, forcing the boat to retire submerged.

The Tirante was still looking for targets on 6 April, just south of the Korean peninsula. No matter where it went, all the crew could find were fishing boats. Street figured the fishermen must know the area well, so he decided to surface and take several prisoners. The Tirante surfaced next to a very frightened group of Korean fisherman—but as it turned out, the fishermen were more frightened of being drafted for military service by the Japanese than being captured by the Americans.

Torpedo Attack #3

Still just south of Korea on 7 April, Street ordered a submerged approach on a brand new 2800-ton freighter. The closeness of the islands in the area wouldn't allow him to make long-range shots.

As the target approached 600 yards, two torpedoes were sent its way. Both hit, and the rush was on in the conning tower. The captain wanted good pictures of the sinking ship, but by the time they got the camera out, the freighter was already on its way to the bottom.

Torpedo Attack #4

After another day of dodging fishing nets, the watch spotted an escorted two-ship convoy on the horizon. In order to get a good radar fix, Street had to expose four feet of periscope. The captain commented that showing that much scope in such glassy seas with escorts all about made them feel like "Lady Godiva in the marketplace!" A close inspection showed the two ships to be a transport and a freighter, both of good size. The Tirante managed to close the range, and Street kept his bow pointed at the escorts to reduce the chance of being picked up on sonar.

Finally, at a range of 1600 yards, he fired three shots at the transport and got good bearings on the freighter. Another quick set of calculations was made and checked, and then three more fish were fired at the freighter. The firs two shots hit the transport. She was sinking quickly when the third blew off her bow.

The freighter apparently managed to react in time to avoid the torpedoes. The Tirante went to the bottom (200 feet) and received a good going-over by the three escorts—she was really boxed in. The escorts took turns, with one pinging and listening and the others dropping charges. Finally, they managed to break contact and get away with only a bent propeller. In all, 83 charges were dropped.

Torpedo Attack #5

Street headed south to Quelpart Island, looking for bigger game. About midnight on 14 April, he approached the island from the north. Three hours of surface investigation showed nothing for certain in the harbor area.

Growing impatient, Street said, "let's get this over," and headed into the harbor area. Now, for the first time, the crew could make out ships, and Street put the tracking team to work. All the targets were stopped, so all the tracking team had to do was get the bearings and correct for the current. A test shot was fired to judge the current; it missed just to the right of the largest target.

They corrected their aim to take the current into account and fired a second and third shot. Both hit with a tremendous explosion. "A great mushroom of white blinding flame shot 2000 feet into the air." They had hit the jackpot—a munitions ship.

With the bright fire burning, the Tirante stood out like a "snowman in a coal mine," so Street ordered full rudder and all ahead flank, but when two freighters came into view, he quickly belayed the order. Two torpedoes were fired at the first and one at the second. The first went up in a ball of fire and the second quietly sank in great cloud of smoke. "Now let's really get out of here," the captain ordered.

With only one torpedo left, Street received the order to return to Midway for a refit. On the way, the Tirante came across a downed Japanese "Zeke" floating upside down with its crew perched on top. Street attempted to get them to come aboard and even brought up the Korean prisoners to try and convince them, but they would have none of it. Abruptly, the Japanese tossed off their life jackets, jumped into the water, and started to swim away from the sub. When one drowned, that convinced the other two, and they finally decided to take the invitation to be POWs on the Tirante. Lt. Commander Beach was given the honor of sinking the plane single-handedly, which he accomplished with a few rifle shots.

The Tirante was initially credited with sinking eight ships for a total of 30,044 tons. Investigations after the war reduced that number to six ships and only 13,000 tons. As the war drew to an end, targets were becoming harder and harder to come by, so either way it was a great patrol.

Lt. Commander Street was only one eight commanders to sink more than five ships in one patrol.

37 USS Sea Dog 4th Patrol

Commanding the three-ship wolf pack in which the Spadefish had so much success was Commander Earl T. Hydeman in the USS Sea Dog. The Sea Dog also had a good run in the Sea of Japan.

On 27 May 1945, the Sea Dog, along with the Spadefish and the Crevalle, left Guam and pointed their bows toward the Tsushima Strait. After successfully negotiating the minefield, each boat headed toward its assigned area.

Torpedo Attack #1

At 2000, on 9 June, as the Sea Dog was preparing to surface between Sado Shima and Honshu, sonar reported incoming screws. A look through the periscope revealed a 1186-ton freighter following a steady course, with its running lights on. One torpedo fired from short range made quick work of the ship. The Sea Dog surfaced several minutes later amid the lifeboats, and when the lookouts took their posts, another ship was spotted.

Torpedo Attack #2

A quick submerged approach put Captain Hydeman in good firing position. One bow shot was fired and hit. The target reversed course in a cloud of smoke and tried to head a way from the sub. A second torpedo hit just forward of amidships. With a huge explosion, the ship broke in two. The bow and stern each sank separately.

Torpedo Attack #3

Shortly after noon on 11 June, another small freighter steamed into view just south of Oga Hanto. Captain Hydeman tried a submerged approach but couldn't close. The weather came to his aid as a thick fog hung close to the water. Using the fog as cover, he surfaced and sped ahead of the target and then submerged and waited.

When the target finally came into view, one torpedo broke her in two. The freighter sank within a minute.

Torpedo Attack #4

The next day, smoke curls were seen to the north of Nyudo Saki. The Sea Dog submerged and approached at high speed. Four ships in a rough box formation were just rounding the point.

With the ships rapidly heading for shallow water, the captain had to settle for a long-range shot. Three fish were fired from 3200 yards. Only one hit, but it broke the target's back and sent it to the bottom. The rest of the convoy hurried to the safety of the shallows. Captain

Hudeman broke off the approach and headed for deeper water.

Torpedo Attack #5

On 15 June, the watch spotted yet another small freighter. This time, Captain Hydeman took a position close to the shore to prevent the target from making a dash to shallow water. One torpedo fired from 1000 yards was all it took to sink the freighter.

Captain Hydeman next set a course up the coast for Oga Hanto as small boats set out from shore to pick up the survivors.

Torpedo Attack #6

Hydeman probably made his only mistake of the patrol during this sixth attack. As the sub was lying in wait close to shore on 19 June, the watch sighted an unescorted four-ship convoy heading right for the Sea Dog.

The range closed rapidly as the Sea Dog turned to bring the more numerous bow tubes to bear. Two shots were fired at the lead ship and three at the second ship, but due to the short torpedo run, the first ship was hit before the second group of torpedoes were on their way. By the time they could be fired, the ships had changed course and all of the second volley missed.

The first ship sank as a plane approached, and Captain Hydeman considered leaving the area. The sinking ship, however, blocked his way forward. He ordered the sub to 150 feet and tried to turn away toward the beach, but quickly found himself in embarrassingly shallow water.

He grounded her lightly at 116 feet, an incident that won the Sea Dog unofficial credit for the first landing and invasion of the Japanese homeland! The captain was finally forced to back out of the area, a feat performed with admirable depth control by switching the bow and stern plane operators.

In accordance with the plan, Hydeman assembled his group at the north end of the sea off the La Perouse Strait on 22 June. On the night of 24 June, the wolf pack made a high-speed surface run through the strait in cotton-thick fog. Once safely through the straits, they set a course for Pearl Harbor. The triumphant subs arrived on the Fourth of July with the colors flying.

One tragedy marred the event. The USS Bonefish didn't return. She was the last Pacific Fleet sub lost in the war.

38 USS Tang 1ˢᵗ Patrol

The mark of a truly great submarine commander is not a single patrol, but a consistent string of successful outings. One such commander was Dick O'Kane of the USS Tang. O'Kane was arguably the hottest sub skipper of the war.

He first served as "Mush" Morton's executive officer and right-hand man on the USS Wahoo, during which time he received a complete education in approach-and-attack tactics from Morton. They used a unique system in which O'Kane would make all of the periscope observations during the approach and attack, leaving Morton free to plan and con the boat to the best attack position. When O'Kane received his own command on the Tang, there was probably no one better at calling angle-on-the-bow, range, and speed through the scope as shown by his high percentage of hits.

The Tang only went out on five war patrols. One of these—the second—was strictly a rescue mission in which the crew pulled 22 downed Navy aviators out of the water. On the other four patrols, from January 1944 to October 1944, the Tang scored an amazing total of 24 ships sunk for a career total of 93, 824 tons.

What follows is a detailed account of the attacks made by Tang, much of which was taken directly from O'kane's patrol reports to his superiors.

Torpedo Attack #1

Rigorous training was conducted during much of the transit to the assigned patrol area near Truk Island, and after being released from lifeguard duty on 7 February, the Tang began to patrol in earnest.

She patrolled on the surface whenever possible, and when submerged, a constant watch was kept on the scope in hope of sighting enemy ships. O'Kane was granted his wish early on the morning of 17 February.

At 0025 that morning, the watch sighted a convoy on the SJ (surface radar) bearing 305T at a distance of 31,000 yards. It was tracked at 8 1/2 knots on base course 100 degrees, directly into the rising half moon, and zigging 40 degrees every 10 to 14 minutes. As viewed on the radar, excluding side lobes, the convoy was composed of two large ships, a somewhat smaller one believed to be a destroyer, a small escort close ahead, two more escorts on either beam, and two more wide-flanking patrols.

> At 0219, when nearly ahead, with range to convoy 15,000 yards, the starboard flanking escort suddenly appeared at 7000 yards, closing at four knots. We were forced down, deep, and given five depth charges, but his attack was halfhearted and we were able to return to radar depth 15 minutes after he passed by. The convoy was still 9000 yards away and coming on nicely. Our approach from here was quite routine, except for additional depth charges and patrolling escorts. Went back

to periscope depth at 4000 yards, watched leading escort cross conveniently to the opposite bow, the port escort crossing our bow...at 0335 fired a spread of four straight stern shots at near (freighter), range 1500 yards, 80 port track, speed 8 1/2. The first three hit their points of aim in the screws, and the after and forward ends of the midship superstructure. Watched the freighter sinking by the stern amidst milling escorts. She was a split superstructure freighter with details similar to the Mansei Maru, low in the water with bulky deck load.

When she sank, we went to our favorite depth below the 375-foot gradient and cleared the area. Some additional depth charging followed, but none close, and we were able to search with the radar and surface at 0500.

When the Tang was able to surface, Captain O'Kane again tracked the convoy and tried to close submerged, but couldn't achieve a suitable firing range. Bombers were a continual problem over the next several days, and if that weren't enough, rain squalls affected the radar, making it necessary to establish visual identification. Often the contacts turned out to be patrol ships and not freighters.

Torpedo Attack #2

On 22 February:

> Following two such approaches on patrols, (we) found a Kenyo Maru-type (freighter) with escorts on starboard and bow quarter. After tracking this freighter zigging on course 225T for another half hour, we moved into position on his port bow, 4000 yards from the nearest escort. An unpredicted zig required a "dipsy-doodle" to maintain an ideal firing position, but he came on nicely, and at 2349, with a range of 1500, 90 port track, and Tang dead in the water and holding her breath, (we) let him have four torpedoes, spread his length from aft forward by constant TBT bearings. The enemy literally disintegrated under four hits and sank before we had completed 90 degrees of our turn to evade. One escort guessed right and closed at 3000 yards, but these boats

always seem to find a couple of extra knots for such occasions, and we made a sand blower out of him.

Torpedo Attack #3

We still had difficulty in identifying the enemy on radar, and our next approach, in spite of sound, developed into a destroyer at 3500 yards with Tang backing down 1200 yards off her track. Both sea and visibility prevented anything but a defensive attack, so we pulled clear with minimum range 2900 yards. There followed one more approach, a bit more cautious, on what appeared to be a submarine, before we located what apparently was a naval auxiliary, definitely of the Arimasan Maru class. As her leading escort conveniently moved out to 8000 yards, we moved into position on her port bow, stopped, and kept pointed at her with another nice rain squall for a background. As she came on, her guns were plainly visible forward, then aft. At 0120, with range 1400, 90 port track, and gyros around zero, (*we) let her have four torpedoes, spread her length from aft forward. The first two were beautiful hits in her stern and just aft of the stack, but the detonation as the third torpedo hit forward of his bridge was terrific. The enemy ship was twisted, lifted from the water as you would flip a spoon on end, and then commenced belching flame as she sank. The Tang was shaken far worse than by any depth charge we could remember, but a quick check as soon as our jaws came off our chests, showed no damage.

As is usually the case when you hit first, the escorts were befuddled and evasion was simplified.

Torpedo Attack #4

Patrolled on the surface, 150 miles west of Saipan, searching with high periscope and radar. At 1109, sighted smoke bearing 015T and immediately picked up two targets on the SJ at 23,000 and 24,000 yards. With clearing horizon, the enemy was shortly identified as a freighter, a large tanker, and a destroyer. Tracking showed them on course 270, opened to maximum radar range to track.

Contact was suddenly lost but a half-hour run at full power toward their last true bearing located them again, this time on base course 165T. Gathering rain squalls made it apparent that we would do well to maintain contact with the enemy during the remainder of the day, and that the only possibility of destroying both ships lay in night, or night and dawn attacks.

At sunset, the destroyer came into a clear spot, sent several signals on a large searchlight to his convoy, lined them up with the tanker astern, and started off on a course west. The enemy zigs were of the wildest sort, sometimes actually backtracking, but their very wildness was his undoing, for after two hours of tacking, and two more (hours) of approaches on their quarters, with outer doors open for firing on four different occasions, the freighter, a Tatutki Maru-class ship, made one of his super right zigs across our bow. At 2230, when the range was 1400, 95 starboard, gyros around zero, we cold-cocked him with the first three of our usual four torpedoes spread along his length by constant TBT bearings. The ship went to pieces and amidst beautiful fireworks sank before we had completed our turn to evade. The tanker opened fire fore and aft immediately, while the destroyer nearly 3000 yards away, closed (on) the scene rapidly. After helping out any possible survivors with 12 depth charges, she rejoined the tanker.

The destroyer stayed so close to the tanker that for several hours we could distinguish only one ship on radar most of the time. They continued on the same base course but settled down to moderate zigs. Before dawn we were in a position 10,000 yards ahead and 80 miles west of Saipan. Only a change of base course could prevent our attack.

Torpedo Attack #5

At 0548, with gray skies in the east, submerged to radar depth, took a last look at range 7000 yards, then started a submerged approach. Eighteen minutes later the tanker was in sight with an Asashio-type destroyer patrolling very close ahead. As we were then 200 yards from the track, (we) turned and paralleled his base course. At range 2000 yards, the destroyer gave us some bad moments by crossing our bow for the second time, pointing directly at our position. But in an attempt to prevent a repetition of his mistake of the night before, he turned right, passed down the tanker's starboard side to that quarter. He was absolutely dwarfed by the length of the loaded tanker, whose details were plainly visible. She was painted slate gray, comparable only to our Cimarron class, but with bridge and foremast well forward, just behind the bulging bow, which mounted an estimated six-inch gun. Her mainmast was close against her after superstructure which was topped by an extremely large short stack. There were at least 150 uniformed lookouts on our side alone.

A 20-degree zig put us a little close to the track, but as we had already commenced out turn away for a stern shot, we were far from inconvenienced. At 0639, with escort just crossing tanker's stern to the far side, (we) fired four torpedoes, range 500 yards, 90 starboard track, gyros around 180 degrees. The first three hit as aimed, directly under the stack, at the forward end of the after superstructure, and under the bridge. The explosions were wonderful; he sank by the stern in four minutes, and then we went deep and avoided.

With four forward torpedoes left, (we) proceeded towards the lower Bonins, our new patrol area.

Torpedo Attack #6

Patrolled on the surface 180 miles northwest of Saipan, sighted smoke which quickly developed into a four-ship convoy. Tracked them on course 160 until after dark, identifying one as a two-stacker. Remained outside 10,000 yards until after moonset, when radar tracking showed them to be worm-turning on a base course east. Found the two-stacker shortly, astern of the leading freighter and just ahead of a small unidentified vessel.

Escorts on either side of the leading freighter offered no (opportunity to close) the two-stacker from the flank. She was now tracked on a straight 090. A column zig brought the leading freighter across our port bow, so (we) twisted left, steadied, and fired our usual spread of four torpedoes covering the entire length of the two-stacker as he came by, range 1600, gyros near zero, 100 starboard track. All torpedoes, even the one fired at his bow, missed stern as we failed to detect his increasing speed. Had little difficulty evading escorts.

Though disappointed not to destroy this passenger ship, the Horai Maru, there is no use in crying over spilt milk.

The Tang is far from cocky and just as determined as ever.

En route Midway.

The Tang and O'Kane were officially credited with sinking five ships for a total of 21,400 tons during this maiden patrol.

39 USS Tang 3rd Patrol

As mentioned, the Tang's second patrol was strictly a lifeguard/rescue operation. She performed in outstanding fashion, picking up 22 downed aviators while often in gun range of the shore. The best was yet to come, however; her 3rd patrol would go down in submarine history.

She departed Midway for the South China Sea on 12 June 1944 at two-engine speed. On 22 June, she made a submerged passage of the Colnett Strait, just to the south of the Japanese mainland. At 2145 on 25 June, the radar man picked up a large convoy and the Tang commenced tracking.

22227: We were in what at first appeared to be a fortunate position on the convoy's port bow, with a three-day-old moon about to set, but as numerous bow and flanking escorts appeared on the radar screen, it became evident that undetected penetration from the flank would be nearly impossible.

The composition of the convoy, which had been confused by numerous escorts and side lobes, was now clarified with visual sightings. There were at least six large ships, in column sections of two, surrounded by two circular screens of at least six escorts each, and as we later discovered, each section was further escorted ahead and astern.

Torpedo Attack #1

As the quarter escorts were well dispersed, (we) elected to approach from the stern. We passed between them without difficulty, diverged to starboard and avoided a third patrol, and gained a position 2300 yards on the starboard beam of the last section.

The leading ship was a large modern four-mast freighter with high composite superstructure topped by a large short stack, believed to be of the Aobasan Maru class. The second ship was a modern tanker with a large short funnel, similar to the Genyo Maru or Kyoktuto Maru. Both ships were heavily loaded and most probably diesel driven as they did not smoke.

> **2349**: The convoy had settled on a course north at ten knots when we stopped, turned left for straight shots, and fired three torpedoes at the freighter, 120 starboard track, range 2600, spread at his length, followed immediately by a similar spread at the tanker, 100 starboard track, range 2450. All gyros were between 12 and 2 right. Observed two beautiful hits in the stern and amidships of the freighter, timed as our first and third torpedoes. The second was observed to run erratically to the left. The explosions appeared to blow the ship's sides out, and he commenced sinking rapidly. On schedule, our fourth and fifth torpedoes hit under the stack and just forward of the after superstructure of the tanker. His whole

after end blazed up until extinguished as he went down by the stern.

0000: We now had evaded the closest escort at 1400 yards apparently unobserved, so pulled up 7000 yards from the convoy and 5000 yards from where our targets would have been. Their pips had gradually disappeared from the radar screen however, and only a cloud of smoke marked the spot where they sank.

Torpedo Attack #2

0020: Started in for another attack. Our approach was spurned by an escort that closed to 1500 yards as we passed the vicinity of the first attack but unable to see us in the haze of a slight (engine) overload, commenced dropping terrific depth charges. He succeeded in calling out the dogs however and our target, which was first tracked at 10 knots, showed stopped, then a range rate of better than 40 knots closing! We had just time to complete a 90-degree turn when he passed 1600 yards astern. He spotted us, closed for a minute, but our team of overload experts, watching their temperatures, got us rolling at 221/2 knots. Easing off each time he showed a slight angle, we eventually opened to 3400 yards when he illuminated. Hoping to take advantage of the experience of others, we dived a little faster than a rock. Though his searchlight illuminated the bridge diving alarm for our CO, he still did not spot us, and passed well clear.

0200: Now with time to consider, (we) believed the Nagasaki area would be very unhealthy at dawn, two hours hence, so (we) surfaced and rounded the Koshiki Islands where we could guard the southern approaches to the straits.

Torpedo Attack #3

On 26 June:

04224: Shortly after crack of dawn (we) sighted a ship on the SJ (surface radar) at 8000 yards. We were already on his beam but fog and rain permitted a full-power end-around with only occasional glimpses of the enemy. He was a medium-sized, split superstructure freighter, similar to Ehime Maru, tracked at 18 knots hugging the coast. With the freighter obscured by rain, dived 1000 yards off his track, range 7000 yards.

0551: Turned right for a stern shot as the freighter came out of the rain and fired four MK 18 torpedoes, range 1950, 100 starboard track, gyros near 180. The torpedoes were set on six feet as the sea was calm and the loading of the freighter could not be ascertained beforehand. Though we had a zero angle on the boat, two of the torpedoes broached several times, then settled down on a surface run, throwing continuous plumes in the air. Needless to say, the freighter avoided the spread by turning toward. After some gunfire, the freighter took refuge in a cove; we surfaced and made a full power dash to the west, unsighted by a late-arriving patrol boat.

Torpedo Attack #4

On 29 June:

1140: Sighted a freighter to the north on a westerly course. Commenced approach but it soon became apparent that we could not reach an attack position submerged. We therefore opened the range on a diverging course, surfaced, and commenced an end-around, bucking heavy seas. Reduced visibility permitted passing the ship with only occasional glimpses at 15,000 yards.

1160: Having tracked the enemy on course 225 at seven knots, dived directly on his track for periscope attack. The freighter came on nicely, identified as the Tanzan Maru, her mast had been cut off level with the top of the stack, but all other details were as shown. He was lightly loaded but in view of our experience of 27 June, decided that ten feet was the absolute minimum depth setting for this sea. After two "dipsy doodles" to adjust position, bearings checked.

1759: Fired two MK 14 torpedoes, one at his foremast and one at his mainmast, 90-degree port track, range 1250 yards, speed 7. Raised periscope again to see the smoke of each torpedo as it (reached its) point of aim, but they apparently passed under.

The enemy turned toward and gave us two close depth charges shortly after we reached two hundred feet, 50 feet off the bottom. Fifteen minutes later, as we were approaching periscope depth, a loud crackling noise came over sound followed by a third fairly close charge.

1910: We went back down, but searched and surfaced 15 minutes later with nothing in sight. This points to the possibility that this last was a delayed-action depth charge used in this shallow water for the purpose of keeping a submarine down while the ship escapes.

2030: It didn't work in this case, however, for we made radar contact in a little over an hour and commenced tracking again. We closed sufficiently to identify him and then turned the tracking over to the section on watch with the plan to attack after moonset in the lee of the Daikokusan Gunto (island).

Torpedo Attack #5

On 30 June:

The freighter was a little out in his navigation; however, his track crossed 15 miles north of the islands. As firing in the lee was not possible and the seas rougher still, (we were) determined to attack from a range to insure hits even with broaching torpedoes.

0040: Commenced approach from his starboard bow, directly down wind and sea, stopped with a range 1500 yards, angle on the bow 40 starboard.

0101: Killed headway as he came on, and fired an MK 14 "feeler" torpedo set on six feet from number 5 tube, range 750 yards, 92 starboard track, 60degree left ran perfectly, its phosphorescent track visible among the white caps right to the freighter's side. The explosion amidships, just 30 seconds after firing, was as beautiful as it was reassuring.

It broke the freighter's back, his stern sinking with a down angle, his forward section with an up, in a cloud of fire smoke and steam.

His gun crew had guts, however, and got off five or six shots in spite of the tilting platform. When they had ceased firing, we relieved about 20 lookouts in rapid succession, and today our crew is discussing single- versus multiple-torpedo fire. We'll continue to fire as many as considered necessary to sink the enemy.

0130: Proceeded north for submerged patrol after daylight.

Torpedo Attack #6

1015: Commenced tracking smoke which quickly developed into two columns, and then the masts of two ships. One ship was zigging at intervals of 3 to 12 minutes, while the other's movements indicated an escort. After gaining position ahead and tracking these ships on a SE course 260 at eight knots, (we) dived for periscope approach and attack.

1322: As the group came on, maneuvered for an MK 18 stern shot at the escort who was about 1500 yards on the freighter's starboard bow. This placed us directly ahead of the freighter and insured a stern shot at him if the escort was not hit. The escort was now identified as small engine-aft freighter with gun forward and depth charges aft. As TDC bearings were lagging, took several echo ranges and found his speed had increased to ten knots.

1444: Now, with the setup checking, fired two MK 18 torpedoes, one under his foremast, the other under his stack, 100 port track, range 1250, depth setting six feet, then went ahead standard speed to gain position on the freighter.

As the moments dragged out and time for the torpedoes to hit apparently passed, (we) expressed some quiet oaths about electric torpedoes, only to have the words jammed down our throats by a swell explosion. Slowed and looked to see the escort's stern in the air in a cloud of smoke, and the freighter turning back. At least a half-dozen persons observed this ship sink, timed in two minutes and 20 seconds.

Torpedo Attack #7

We now felt that we had the freighter caught between third base and home, for he was nearly 100 miles from the Korean coast and his track led through the probable position of both the USS Sea Lion and the USS Tinosa. Sent them contact report on next hourly schedule and continued trailing submerged at five knots.

1916: With smoke still in sight, surfaced at dusk and commence overtaking at full power on three engines, charging (batteries) with the other. After radar contact with the enemy had been gained, it became apparent that we would have to pass him up moon south of Ko To, but with full power on four engines, we were waiting for him with two minutes to spare as he approached the southern tip of the island.

2224: Dived a mile and a half off the island, 1200 yards north of the track of the enemy who was now 6000 yards away. He showed from 11 to 9 knots as he passed the southern tip, but with three echo ranges and periscope bearings, the setup was checking again and we commenced our turn for a straight bow shot. With range 500, 90-degree port track, gyros near zero, fired two MK 14 torpedoes by constant bearings, the first at the middle of his after well deck, the second at the middle of his forward one. The first torpedo hit as aimed in 20 seconds, exploding the ship's cargo which must have been munitions of some sort. A short section of the bow was all that remained intact of the whole ship, and it sank in 20 seconds. The second torpedo was "robbed."

Torpedo Attack #8

On 4 July:

0408: As the sky was overcast at dawn, (we) continued on the surface, and shortly sighted heavy masts of a ship to the northeast.

(We) stopped, put him astern, and determined his approximate southerly course, and commenced full power dash to get on his track. We were a bit hampered by 15 trawlers or fisherman , but with the enemy's bridge and stack aft already over the horizon, it was their presence that prevented our detection.

0506: With angle on the bow five starboard, (we) dived and continued our approach. The massiveness of the ship as it closed resembled a man-of-war, and 20 minutes later a wide zig gave us our first good identification look. Her hull and arrangement were similar to Kurosio Maru, with modifications. During the next hour, we were abaft of his beam as he closed the ten-fathom curve, zigging leisurely. On our straight course at full speed we closed the range continuously however, and though on most observations with angles on the bow up to 150 degrees the situation looked hopeless, he finally reached the nine-fathom finger west of Ama To and came back to a southerly course. Our fathometer, which had been allowing four fathoms under our keel, now in quick succession showed three, two, then merged with the outgoing signal.

0626: So we backed down and fired three MK 14 torpedoes at stack, amidships, and forward, by constant bearings, range 2600, 90 starboard track, speed 8, depth setting eight feet. Turned left with full speed and rudder, and heard healthy hits timed as our first and second torpedoes. We slowed and looked to see only the bow, stern, and mast sticking out of the water under a huge cloud of smoke.

Torpedo Attack #9

1840: Having passed Osei To, (we) sighted smoke beyond the Oiyono group of islands, tracked on a southerly course. While figuring out where and how we could get him under a full moon in more than ten fathoms, our problem was solved by a faint wisp of smoke to the west.

(We) switched approach to this and closed at standard speed submerged until clear of Osei To.

1953: Then surfaced in late twilight, but under a full moon. Twenty minutes later he was sighted on the radar at 18,500 yards. We were in a fortunate position ahead and only had to move on to his base course of 110 which led to Osei To. His long silhouette was visible at 15,000 yards, so (we) tracked from that range, determining his moderate zigs of 20 to 30 degrees at five to ten minute intervals.

2041: Dived and tracked enemy by radar to 9000 yards, then commenced moonlight periscope attack.

As he came on, his silhouette developed into a long engines-aft ship with raked bow, and with tripod mast and king posts forward and aft.

Distinctive also was his mushroom-topped bridge structure.

2128: After closing the left zig at standard speed, checked set up with several echo ranges, and fired last two bow torpedoes, range 900 yards, 90-degree starboard track, gyros near zero, depth setting eight feet. The first torpedo hit just aft of the bridge, breaking the ship's back. The tripod foremast could be seen through the smoke, and debris tilting aft as she sank by the middle. Let crew hear the breaking-up noises by the sound-1MC method, then surfaced to pick up a survivor. It was necessary to snake one of the large overturned lifeboats alongside with grapples, and threaten with tommy gun bursts the one visible survivor to (convince him to) come on aboard. Recovering a life ring was much easier.

Both the new life boats and life ring, and visual observation of the vessel before firing show this to have been a new ship.

Torpedo Attack #10

On 5 July:

2257: When eight miles west of Choppeki Point, after having tracked one side lobe, and investigated several second pulse echoes, (we) sighted a ship on the SJ at 29,000 yards. Stopped and tracked it out to 32,000 on a northwesterly course at nine knots, then commenced a grueling end-around.

0227: Stopped on his track seven miles ahead for final speed and course check, then dived on a parallel course for a submerged attack. Checked the setup by radar observation at 5000 yards when the freighter was temporarily lost in the surface haze, and immediately experienced hopelessly fogging periscopes. The setup checked perfectly, however, showing us 500 yards off the track, so returned to 60 feet to wet the scopes. He was clear and big on the next observation at 1100 yards by echo range.

0320: So turned for the stern shot. Fired two MK 18 torpedoes, one at his mainmast, one at his foremast, range 900 yards, 90-degree starboard track, depth setting six feet. Both torpedoes hit exactly as aimed, and there was only broken wreckage and floating life boats in sight when we surfaced two minutes later.

0325: As two pips at 16,000 yards were closing, perhaps belated escorts, and sky already pink, commenced full power run to south. Dived 50 miles from attack.

At noon, on 14 July, the Tang arrived back at Midway Island.

The USS Tang and Commander O'Kane were eventually credited with sinking ten ships on this patrol, although he initially claimed only eight. The official tonnage mark was 39,100 tons. This patrol was tops for the war in number of ships sunk, and only topped by three others in the most tonnage sunk on a single patrol. The three skippers that beat O'Kane sank far fewer ships but were each fortunate enough to score one really large hit.

Based on this performance, Richard O'Kane can lay claim to the title of the war's best sub commander, but he was by no means finished.

40 USS Tang 4th Patrol

O'Kane said the refit received at Midway from SubDiv 62 and Submarine Base Midway was the finest to date, and by 31 July, he was underway again to patrol Empire waters.

Torpedo Attack #1

On 10 August:

> **1010**: having avoided another patrol by continuing in, (we) sighted an odd-type loaded tanker against the beach, headed for Omai Saki

(off the southeastern shore of Japan). As four bombers were the only escorts, standard speed approach closed him to 120 yards where with echo and stadimeter ranges checking, fired three MK 23 torpedoes spread on his length, 100 starboard track, speed 8.5, set at eight feet, gyros near zero. No hits, or explosions on the beach three thousand yards away, resulted. Two minutes after firing the tanker, alerted, reversed course away, so commenced evasion, thoroughly expecting bombs or aerial depth charges. We rolled on the bottom a little at 80 feet during our turn to evade, but reached deep water and commenced periscope patrol in another hour.

Torpedo Attack #2

On 11 August:

0413: Having doubled back Miki Saki, (we) dived three miles west of the point, then closed to intercept any morning shipping.

1065: Sighted smoke.

1635: Smoke, which had been in two columns, developed into two freighters in column. They were escorted well to seaward by the gunboat previously sighted, and by a smaller escort on the other bow. During the remainder of the approach, the leading ship was identified as of the Biyo Maru class, and the second about two-thirds her size. Both ships were heavily loaded.

1740: When in position 1700 yards off the convoy's beam, just prior to giving a final setup, sound reported fast screws on our port quarter. A quick look showed our gunboat coming in fast a thousand yards away.

1741: Fired three MK 23 torpedoes at the leading freighter range 1800, 110 starboards track, depth setting six feet, spread 150 percent of the target's length, followed by a similar spread at the second freighter on an 80 starboard track. Took a quick low-power sweep to observe the gunboat filling the field, boiling past our stern evidently having misjudged our course and giving the wrong lead. Reassured, (we) swung quickly to the leading target in time to see the first torpedo hit right in the middle, evidently in his Scotch boilers, for he disintegrated with the explosion.

1743: On our way deep, timed our fourth and fifth torpedoes to hit the second freighter, followed by a tooth-shaking depth charge attack. The gunboats' screws on our port side showed his intent to turn us toward shallow water; (we) made a full speed dash. Even at this speed, the twisting, scrunching, breaking-up noises were loud in the direction of the targets.

1821: After 22 close ones, the depth charges drew aft and we were able to return to periscope depth in 38 minutes. The gunboat was now about 4000 yards on our quarter, the other escort at the scene of the attacks apparently picking up survivors, and one plane was circling the area. Nothing else was in sight.

Torpedo Attack #3

20 August:

0947: Sighted tops and smoke of a freighter coming out of the mist from the north. As the enemy was still inside the ten-fathom curve, we still had to close the coast a little and dodge sampans, but his escorts were well clear on his beam and port bow to seaward. The freighter was a modern medium-sized aft-engine ship. With range 900, 123 port track, speed 8, gyros around 30, (we) fired two MK 23 torpedoes at his stack and foremast.

The first torpedo evidently missed astern and exploded on the beach, while the second torpedo left the tube with a clonk but did not run.

We had to take our first eight depth charges at periscope depth but had gained deep water for the next 22.

Torpedo Attack #4

21 August:

0855: A large ship and two escorts proceeded eastward, and rounding Shiono Misaki, we closed the next freighter two hours later. She was a medium-sized new engine-aft job with escorts well ahead, but with a 3000-yards torpedo run, (we) broke off the attack as a better shot was practically assured.

1243: (We) sighted smoke, then a medium-sized freighter coming up the coast unbelievably close to the beach. Our approach mainly consisted of ducking the two subchasers and whale killer escorts, and turning left for a stern shot.

1317: At a range of 1650 yards, (we) fired three MK 18 torpedoes spread 150 percent of the freighter's length, 110 port track, gyros around 20 left. All torpedoes exploded on the beach.

We were at 200 feet when the first depth charges came. Our evasion kept everything aft, including late-arriving pingers. Checks on the firing bearings with our MK 18, and plot of the firing showed everything in order. This left only the possibility of deep-running torpedoes to explain our persistent misses, so decided to keep slugging and continue checking torpedoes.

1916: On surfacing, proceeded clear to probe the above bay.

Torpedo Attack #5

On 22 August:

0020: After crossing Miki Saki, slowed, crossed the 100-fathom curve, and proceeded around Kuki Saki. Side lobes were confusing, but we soon found "a pip where no pip ought to be." The night was black and only the long shape of the enemy could be seen until we circled him to get away from the land background. There he was quite visible, identified as the gunboat who had harassed us on our first visit, topping it off with those "tooth shakers." He tracked at zero speed and was obviously anchored in about 20 fathoms, two miles northwest of Kuki Saki. Holding our breath, we moved slowly to 1200 yards, twisted, then steadied for a straight stern shot.

0142: Fired one MK 18 torpedo at his middle set on three feet. The phosphorescent wake petered out after a hundred yard run with the torpedo evidently heading down, and hit the bottom with a loud rumble, timed half way to the enemy, where there should have been 250 feet of water. It was tracked by sound to this moment, but after the rumble cleared away, nothing more was heard.

0144: Fired a second MK 18 torpedo set on three feet, feeling sure the enemy had been alerted by the first. Its wake was dimly visible directly to the target, tracked also by sound, but it passed underneath, apparently running on the deep side, too.

0158: With one salvo of three left aft, (we) circled for a bow shot, and with range 900, fired a MK 23 torpedo from number 5 tube at his middle, set on zero feet. Though we were stopped and absolutely steady and the gyro angle zero, it took a 30-yard jog to the left before settling down towards the target, missing aft.

0200: Still whispering, though the first two torpedoes must have roared past him, (we) fired a second MK 23 from number 6 tube, set on zero, aimed at his gun forward. It took a job to the left also but settled down right for his middle. The explosion 400 seconds later was the most spectacular we've ever seen, topped by a pillar of fire and more explosions about 500 feet in the air. There was absolutely nothing left of the gunboat.

Feeling that our difficulties had been mainly in sluggish steering and depth engines, (we) withdrew at full power to spend the day checking afterbodies of our remaining torpedoes.

1900: Now confident that our last two salvos would count, (we) headed for Omai Saki and the scene of our first attack of the patrol.

Torpedo Attack #6

1017: With a destroyer just clear, the reason for the activity became apparent with the sighting of masts and superstructure of a ship coming down the coast. He was escorted by a destroyer ahead, and escorts on his bow and astern.

We had been forced out a little by the destroyer, and a high-speed approach was necessary to insure a short firing range. It was therefore not until the angle on the bow opened ten minutes later that the full import of our enemy became apparent. The decks of his long superstructure were lined with men in white uniforms as was his upper bridge.

1116: Another five-minute dash to close the track, (we) slowed and took two echo ranges, and fired three MK 23 torpedoes spread along his length, 105 starboard track, range 800 yards, speed 8, depth setting six feet. Then commenced swinging for a stern shot at the rear LST. The first and third torpedoes hit beautifully giving him a 20-degree down angle which he maintained as he went under with naval ensign flying.

For once, depth charging the submarine seemed to take second priority, undoubtedly as survivors were being picked up, for it was 20 minutes before they started to rain. We had then reached deep water and two hours at high speed left everything astern.

1907: Following our hit-and-run policy, commenced a full-power dash to round Shiono Misaki for another crack at the coastal traffic before a waxing moon made evasion difficult.

On 25 August:

1135: Smoke appeared around Miki Saki. The tops, now visible, developed into a medium freighter. Guessing that they would continue across, we turned for a stern shot with our last torpedoes. The (turned) into a narrow bay however, giving us a 130-degree port track with a range between 1500 and 2000 yards. Confident we could do better, and influenced a little by an escort about to take off our periscope, (we) broke off the attack.

Torpedo Attack #7

1715: Two, then three, patrols swept the area, followed by a distant high-frequency echo ranging from down the coast. It grew steadily louder until four escort vessels were in sight. The coast was obscured by passing rain but soon the enemy ship came in sight, very close to the beach.

1743: She presented a starboard angle, so (we) closed on the beach to get on her track before turning off for a stern shot. On the next observation, we were on her port bow (and) so came to the reverse of her course for low-parallax firing.

The enemy was now identified as a modern, medium-sized diesel tanker, heavily loaded. Her quarter escort dropped astern as she came on; three others remained fanned out on her starboard bow, while a fifth ranged ahead. Our navigator was correct when he tabooed turning for a straight stern shot, for our first echo range showed 800 yards to the beach.

The second on the enemy, checked with the periscope stadimeter at 600 yards, so using constant bearings, (we) fired the first MK 18 torpedo at his stern, the second amidships, and the last (one-third ship length ahead, right for the middle of the three escorts nearly in a line-of-bearing on his starboard bow. Though the depth was six feet and the gyros around 60 degrees, the first two hit exactly as aimed, and the third just blew the heck out of the leading escort.

1808: What was left of the tanker had now sunk and the stern escort was making a run toward where his quarter would have been. The enemy obviously never knew where the torpedoes had come from, and though his search became systematic with a total of 68 depth charges, our 100-turn evasion outflanked him.

2039: With the moon hidden, (we) surfaced and cleared the area.

On 6 August, the crew "headed for Pearl."

In his report to his commander, O'Kane said they would have come back with a "fuller bag" had it not been for the torpedo performance problems. Still, he could claim sinking five ships for a total of more than 30,000 tons.

The post war investigation clearly did a disservice to O'Kane and company. Although he had seen most of the freighters from torpedo attack #2 and the large transport from torpedo attack number #6. His official total was reduced to 11,463.

41 USS Tang: 5th Patrol and Loss of the Tang

The training and leadership of Commander O'Kane paid off handsomely in the Tang's 5th and final patrol. Never was there a patrol executed so well that ended so tragically. Of 24 torpedoes fired, 23 hit their targets. Ironically, the twenty-fourth hit the Tang, causing her loss.

The patrol began as usual with the Tang leaving Midway to patrol the Formosa Straits on 27 September 1944. Normal training was carried out en route, and by the time the Tang arrived on station, the officers and crew were primed for action. They didn't have long to wait.

Torpedo Attack #1

On 11 October:

> **0400**: Made radar contact at 17,000 yards on a ship moving up the coast from Pakusa Point. Tracked him at 14 knots making us at first suspicious of his character, but as the range closed he was observed to be a large modern diesel freighter heavily loaded, presenting a low silhouette. We moved onto his track and dived for one of those never-failing crack-of-dawn attacks. Maneuvered for an 800-yard shot as he came by and fired three MK 18 bow torpedoes, spread his length. The first two hit exactly as aimed sinking this overloaded ship immediately. Surfaced as soon as the smoke had cleared to find no survivors. Dived off of Pakusa Point where a north-or south-bound ship could be spotted coming in either direction, permitting a submerged attack if necessary, but preferably

tracking until dark as these shallow waters cramped any ordinary evasion tactics.

Torpedo Attack #2

1000: Masts of another north-bound freighter were sighted down the coast. He was running inside the ten-fathom curve and zigging frequently. Though we could reach his track by moving in at high speed and have some battery left for evasion, our original plan of tracking till dark seemed more prudent under the circumstances. Our tracks converged and he passed directly over us at sundown.

After dark, (we) surfaced 4000 yards astern of him, passed him at the same range, avoided a couple of stationary patrols, moved on to his track, then turned off for a stern shot as he came by.

2100: With a salvo of three ready to fire with a liberal spread, fired a single MK 18 torpedo at his middle with practically zero gyro, on a 75-port track, range 500. Our experience of this morning was not a mistake. We were clicking and this one hit with a terrific explosion. One the first few members of the fire control party to reach the bridge saw any of the ship before it went down.

Proceeded down the coast avoiding two stationary patrols.

On 23 October:

0300: On the first trial of the revamped SJ the operator reported land at 14,000 yards where no land ought to be. Commenced tracking immediately, discovering a small pip moving out in our direction. Put him astern and bent on the turns. He evidently lost his original contact with us for he changed course and commenced a wide sweep about the convoy which was now in sight.

A submariner's dream quickly developed as we were able to assume the original position of the destroyer just ahead of the convoy while he went on a 20-mile inspection tour. The convoy was composed of three large modern tankers in a column, a transport on the starboard hand, a freighter on the north hand, flanked by DEs on both flanks and quarters.

After zigging with the convoy in position 3000 yards ahead, we dropped back between the tankers and the freighter. On next zig, we stopped and turned right for nearly straight bow shots at the tankers as they came by, firing two torpedoes under the stack and engine room space of the nearest tanker, a single torpedo shot into the protruding stern of the middle tanker, and two torpedoes under the stack and engine space of the far tanker. The minimum range was 300 yards and the maximum 800. Torpedoes were exploding before the firing was completed and all hit as aimed. It was a terrific sight to see three blazing, sinking tankers, but there was only time for just a glance as the freighter was in position crossing our stern.

Completed my setup and was about to fire on this vessel when Leibold, my boatswain's mate, whom I've used for an extra set of eyes on all patrols, properly diagnosed the maneuvers of the starboard transport coming in like a destroyer aiming to ram. We were boxed in by the sinking tankers, the transport was too close for us to dive, so we had to cross his bow. It was really a thriller-diller with the Tang barely getting on the inside of his turning circle and saving the stern with full left rudder in the last seconds.

The transport commenced firing with large and small caliber stuff, so (we) cleared the bridge before realizing that it was all over our heads. A quick glance aft, however, showed that the tables were again turning, for the transport was forced to continue her swing in an attempt to avoid colliding with the freighter which had also been coming in to ram. The freighter struck the transport's starboard quarter shortly after we commenced firing four stern torpedoes spread along their double length. At a range of 400 yards, the crash coupled with the four torpedo explosions was terrific, sinking the freighter nose down almost instantly while the transport hung with a 30 degree up angle.

The destroyer was now coming in on our starboard quarter at 1300 yards with DEs on our port bow and beam. We headed for the DE on our bow so as to get the destroyer astern, and gratefully watched the DE turn away, apparently having seen enough. Our destroyer still hadn't lighted off another boiler and it was possible to open range slowly, avoiding the last interested DE. When radar range to the DD was 4500 yards, he gave up the chase and returned to the scene of the transport. We moved back also as (the transport's) bow still showed on radar.

When we were 6000 yards off, however, another violent explosion took place and the bow disappeared from sight and the radar screen. The explosion set off a gun duel amongst the destroyer and escort vessels who fired at random, sometimes apparently at each other and sometimes just out into the night. Their confusion was truly complete. It looked like a good place to be away from so we cleared the area at full power until dawn.

On 24 October:

0600: Convoy sighted. The staff had been correct in their estimate of the situation that the Japanese would likely send every available ship in support of the Philippine campaign. The Leyte Campaign was in progress and the ships of this convoy, as in the one of 23 October, were all heavily loaded. The tankers all carried planes on deck, and even the bows and sterns of the (ships) were piled high with apparent plane crates.

Torpedo Attack #3

The convoy was tracked on a course following the ragged coast at 12 knots. The Japanese became suspicious during our initial approach, two escorts commenced to run on opposite course to the long column, firing bursts of 40mm and five-inch salvos.

As we continued to close the leading ships, the escort commander obligingly illuminated the column with a searchlight, using it to signal. It gave us a perfect view of our first selected target, a three-deck, tow-stack transport the second target, a three-decker one-stacker; and of the third, a large, modern tanker.

With ranges from 1400 yards on the first transport to 900 yards on the tanker, (we) fired two MK 18 torpedoes each in slow, deliberate salvos to pass under the foremast and mainmast of the first two vessels, and under the middle and mainmast of the first two vessels, and under the middle and stack of the tanker. In spite of the apparent early warning and sporadic shooting which was apparently designed to scare the submarine, no evasive tactics were employed by any of the ships. The torpedoes commenced hitting as we paralleled the convoy to search out our next two targets.

Our love for the MK 18 torpedoes after the disappointing cruiser experience was again restored as all torpedoes hit nicely. We passed the next ship, a medium freighter, a beam at 600 yards and then turned for a stern shot at another tanker and transport astern of her.

(We) fired a single stern torpedo under the tanker's stack and one at the foremast and one at the mainmast of the transport. The ranges were between 600 and 700 yards. Things were anything but calm and peaceful now, for the escorts had stopped their warning tactics and were directing good salvos at us and the blotches of smoke we left behind on going to full power to pull clear of the melee.

Just after firing at the transport, a full-fledged destroyer charged under her stern and headed for us. Just exactly what took place in the net few seconds will never be determined, but the tanker was hit nicely and blew up, apparently a gasoline-loaded job. At least one torpedo was observed to hit the transport and an instant later, the destroyer blew up, either intercepting our third torpedo or possibly (a casualty of) the 40mm fire from the two DEs bearing down on our beam. In any case, the result was the same and only the transport remained afloat and she apparently stopped.

We were as-yet untouched, all the gunfire either having cleared over our heads or being directed at several blurbs of smoke we emitted when pleading for more speed. When 10,000 yards from the transport, we were all in the clear so (we) stopped to look over the situation and recheck our last two torpedoes which had been loaded forward during our stern tube attack.

A half-hour was spent with each torpedo,... .drawing it from the tube, ventilating the battery, and checking the rudders and gyros. With everything in readiness, (we) started cautiously back in to get our cripple. The two DEs were patrolling on his seaward side, so (we) made a wide sweep and came in very slow so as not to be detected even by sound. She was lower in the water but not definitely sinking. Checked our speed by pit log at six knots, fired our twenty-third torpedo from 900 yards, aimed just forward of her mainmast. Observed the phosphorescent wake heading as aimed at our crippled target, fired our twenty-fourth and last torpedo at his foremast. Rang up emergency speed as this last torpedo broached and curved sharply to the left.

(We) completed part of a fishtail maneuver in a futile attempt to clear the turning circle of this erratic circular run. The torpedo was observed through about 180 degrees of its turn due to the phosphorescence of its wake. It struck abreast of the after torpedo room with a violent explosion about 20 seconds after firing. The tops were blown off the only regular ballast tanks aft and the after three compartments flooded instantly. The Tang sank by the stern. There was insufficient time to carry out the last order to close the hatch. One consolation for those of us washed off into the water was the explosion of our twenty-third torpedo and observation of our last target settling by the stern.

As O'Kane was washed into the water, what actually happened below during the Tang's last few minutes was described after the war by the nine survivors.

The explosion was very violent, breaking air lines, lifting deck plates, and so forth. Men as far forward as the control room suffered broken limbs and other injuries. The immediate result to the ship was to flood the after three compartments together with the number 6 and number 7 ballast tanks. No one escaped from these compartments and even the forward engine room was half flooded before the after door could be secured. The steep down angle caused all in the conning tower to fall aft, preventing them from closing the hatch.

In the control room, the men succeeded in closing the conning tower hatch, but it had been jimmied in the explosion and leaked badly. They then leveled the boat out ob flooding the number two main ballast tank, and proceeded to the forward torpedo room carrying the injured in blankets.

When the survivors of the forwards engine room and after battery compartments reached the mess room, they found water already above the eye port in the door to the cont4rol room. On testing higher, up by the ventilation pipes, they found the water had not yet reached that high, so they opened the door, letting the water rush through, then proceeded to the forward torpedo room. This made total of about 30 to reach an escape position.

Escape was delayed by the presence of Japanese patrol boats occasionally dropping depth charges. This was unfortunate as an electrical fire in the forward battery compartment was becoming severe. Commencing at about 1800, four parties left the ship. At the time the last party escaped, the forward battery fire had reached such intensity that paint on the forward torpedo room bulkhead was scorching and running down.

Considerable pressure had built up in the battery room making it difficult to secure the door sufficiently tight to prevent acrid smoke from seeping by the gasket. The door gasket probably blew out, either owing to the pressure or as a result of an ensuing battery explosion. The remaining men were probably asphyxiated.

Of the thirteen men who escaped, five were able to cling to the buoy until picked up. Three others reached the surface but weren't able to hang on or breathe. They floated off and drowned. The other five were not seen after leaving the escape trunk.

Of the nine officers and men on the bridge, three were able to swim through the night and until picked up eight hours later, this included Lt. Commander O'Kane. One officer escaped from the flooded conning tower and remained afloat until rescue with the aid of his trousers converted into a life belt.

The destroyer escort that picked up all nine survivors was one of four rescuing Japanese troops and personnel. "When we realized that our clubbings and kickings were being administered by the survivors of our own handiwork, we found that we could take it with less prejudice."

Only four of these brave men, again including O'Kane, were ultimately recovered from Japanese POW camps after the war.

And so ended the amazing career of the USS Tang. She was officially credited with sinking seven ships for 22,000 tons of this last patrol.

Glossary of Terms

Aft
Near or toward the back of a boat or ship.

Amidships
Near or toward the middle of a boat or ship.

Angle on the bow
The direction the target is traveling relative to the submarine. An Angle on the bow of 0 0 means dive deep, you're in trouble.

Beam
The width of a vessel; as, one vessel is said to have more beam than another.

Bearing
The direction you are looking, either through your binoculars or the scope.

Bow
The forward part of a boat or ship.

COMSUBPAC
Commander of Submarines Pacific Fleet.

DD
Designation for a destroyer.

DE
Designation for a destroyer escort.

Dive bubble
Indicator used to measure the angle of a dive.

Dive planes
Large metal wing-like structures located for and aft used to force the bow up or down to surface or dive.

Exec or XO
Executive Officer, second in command aboard a ship or submarine.

Fathom
A unit of measuring depth equal to six feet.

Gyro

A gyroscopic device inside U.S. torpedoes, which enables them to be set to travel on a specified angle, or course, after leaving the sub.

Heading

The direction of a ship's travel measured in degrees from 0 (true north) to 359.

Keel

The main support of a ship, which extends its entire length, frequently used to describe a ship's bottom.

Knot

Unit of speed on ships equal to one nautical mile (6080.27 feet) per hour.

Line of sight

An imaginary line from your position to another object.

Magnetic detonator

A device used in some U.S. torpedoes that measures a change in magnetic fields. It could cause a torpedo to explode if it passed under the keel of a ship.

Mark
A term used during target tracking, meaning take an instrument reading now.

Maru
Japanese term for merchant ship.

Port
The left side of a ship when facing forward.

Rudder
A plane mounted vertically on a ship's stern, used to change the ship's heading or direction.

SJ
Surface radar.

Sonar
A method of locating and measuring the range of objects in water by sending out a sound signal, listening for a reflection of that signal of an object (ship or sub), and measuring the time interval between sending the signal and receiving back the reflected signal. Also, sometimes used to mean listening passively for sounds with a hydrophone—a device for picking up sounds underwater.

Starboard

The right side of a ship when facing forward.

Stern

The rear of a boat or ship.

TBT

Target-bearing transmitter, which consisted of a pair of binoculars mounted to a device on the bridge of a sub. The device transmitted to the torpedo data computer the direction the binoculars were pointing.

TDC

This was a mechanical, analog-computing device used in subs to solve the target tracking equation when given a set of input data concerning the target range, heading, and speed. Once a firing solution was determined, it would automatically transmit the proper gyro setting to the torpedoes.

Test depth

The maximum known safe depth a submarine hull can withstand. Taking a sub deeper than this test depth was dangerous, but sometimes conditions required it.

Thermocline
Also Temperature Gradient and Layer. Refers to the dividing line between layers of water of different temperatures. Once below this layer, a submarine is difficult to find with sonar due to the sound-reflective nature of this layer.

Track
A line referring to a course or line of travel.

Trim
The process of moving water in and out of tanks to stabilize the submarine at a given depth.

Ultra
A secret radio message giving sub commanders the location of enemy convoys. The information in these massages was usually obtained by breaking Japanese radio codes.

Wolf pack
Two or more subs cooperating to attack enemy shipping.

Made in the USA